INVASION KUWAIT
(An Englishwoman's Tale)

JEHAN S. RAJAB

The Radcliffe Press
London · New York

Published in 1993 by
The Radcliffe Press
45 Bloomsbury Square
London WC1A 2HY

175 Fifth Avenue
New York
NY 10010

In the United States of America
and Canada distributed by
St Martin's Press
175 Fifth Avenue
New York
NY 10010

A full CIP record for this book is available from the British Library
A full CIP record is available from the Library of Congress

ISBN 1–85043–775–0

Copy-edited and laser-set by Selro Publishing Services, Oxford
Printed and bound in Great Britain by WBC Ltd, Bridgend, Mid Glamorgan

Invasion Kuwait
(An Englishwoman's Tale)

To the symbol of Kuwait HH the Amir,
Sheikh Jaber Al Ahmad Al Sabah
and
the Crown Prince HH Sheikh Saad Al Abdullah Al Salim Al Sabah

To my son Nadr
and to the *Samideen* in Kuwait during the occupation

To all those who were hostages or were in hiding
and
Kuwait's prisoners-of-war in Iraq
We will not forget them

To the memory of
Dame Violet Dickson

who loved Kuwait and spent over 60 years of her
life there. She was airlifted out along with women
and children after the invasion and passed away
in England never having seen Kuwait liberated.
To me she represented the passing of old Kuwait.

'Whoever might perfume a scorpion
Will not thereby escape its sting.'
— Hadrat Bahaudin Naqshbandi

Contents

Acknowledgements

THERE would have been no journal, book or Kuwait had it not been for the Coalition forces, especially the Americans and the British, who came out to the desert prepared to fight to return Kuwait to its people.

To all the Coalition forces, men and women
God bless you and thank you.

Thank you to members of staff and friends and students who helped clean up the school immediately after the liberation; the following spent a great deal of time working in unpleasant circumstances — Mrs R. Freij, Abu Ali (Khairy Shehab), Gladys Edakattil, Mr Mohammed Sofdar, Mr Tewfiq Salameh, Mrs W. Alfred, Eman and Imani Alfred, Rowa Malik Adaweh, Hamed Al Yassin, Muna Khairy Shehab, Mr Daoud, Nur Hashim Rajab, Taghrid Rasoul and Mrs Pamela Al Bashir.

Thank you to Mrs B. Al Shami and Mr Mohammed Sofdar of the New English School for helping to type this manuscript.

Last, but certainly not least, I would like to express my appreciation to Mr Lester Crook of The Radcliffe Press who was so generous with his time and gave me much valuable advice, some of which I did not take, but most of which I did. Any mistakes are entirely my own.

Glossary of Arabic Terms

abaya (pl. abat)	black silk mantle worn by women
ahlan	welcome
aish Jaber	Long Live Jaber (slogan at Kuwaiti demonstrations)
Allah-u-Akbar	God is Great
attar	perfume
baqala	small local grocery
Basrawiya	woman of Basra, the second town of Iraq
bisht (pl. bishut)	shoulder mantle worn by men, woven from camel hair
chelb Jaber	Jaber's dog
dhuif	guests
dishdasha	long garment falling in a loose straight line from shoulder to ankle
diwaniyas	men's sitting rooms
farwahs	sheepskin winter coats
Hajjia	Haj/Hajjia — one who has made the Haj or pilgrimage to Mecca — honorific title for an older person
harami	thief
hurriyeti	my freedom (vb. hurriye)
Jesh Sha'abi	People's Army — volunteer soldiers
jihad	holy war
jindi	soldier
khubiz Irani	Iranian bread
khubiz Libnani	Lebanese bread

Glossary

kuffiyeh	Arab headdress worn by men
laat khafee	do not be frightened
La-illaha-illa-allah	There is no God save Allah, the One
makhakirah	settlers
memnouh	forbidden
memnouh dish dakhil	it is forbidden to come inside
Mubahath	civil intelligence
mudhif	Marsh Arab guest house built of reeds
Mukhabarat	Secret police — numerous and much feared in Iraq for their brutality
nakhoda	ship's captain
Raees	President
sedu	Bedouin weavings
shehid	martyr
Suq el Hareem	women's market
tefteesh	police inspections — has sinister connotations in Arabic
thawra	revolution
Thawrat-il Zenj	Revolt of the Slaves
thob	long transparent net-like overdress
wanette	A 'pick-up' truck — an Arabized word as the original was an American 'vanette'.

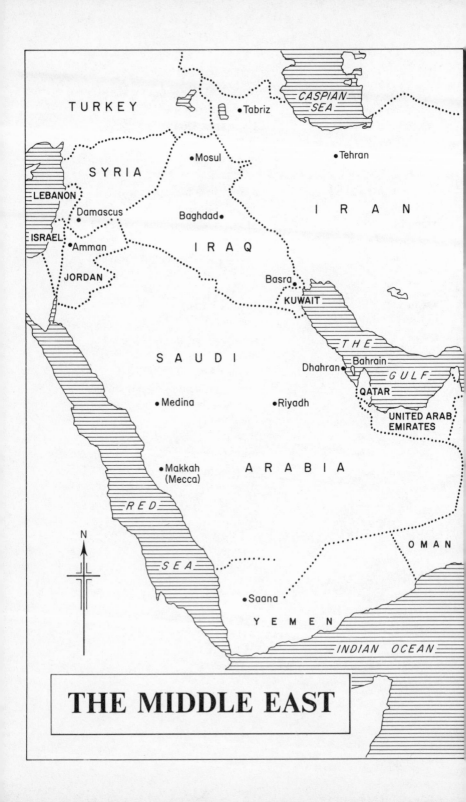

THE MIDDLE EAST

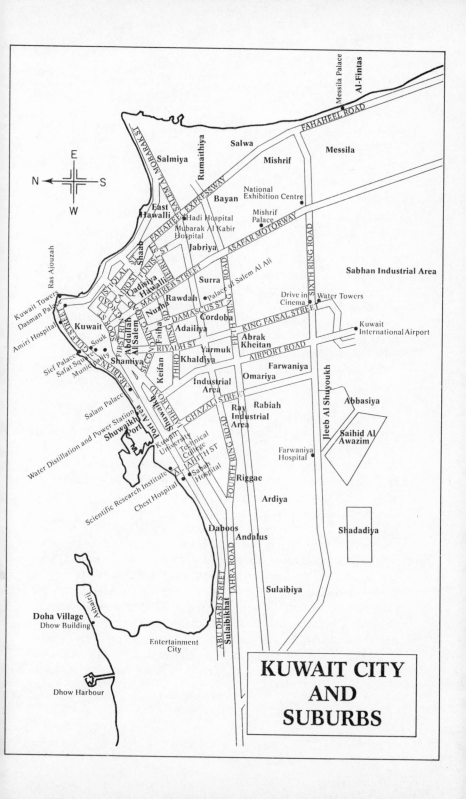

KUWAIT CITY AND SUBURBS

Introduction

W HILE the invasion of Kuwait by Iraq should have begun to fade
into the background after more than two years, I suspect that
for those who were closely involved, including thousands of non-
Kuwaitis, it has not really done so and its effects will never completely
disappear. For Kuwaitis the sense of outrage and betrayal will long
remain. Kuwait's prisoners of war, the hostages, those in hiding and the
refugees might never completely put the legacy of the experience they
suffered behind them.

The whole crisis, from the moment Iraq invaded Kuwait in the early
morning of 2 August 1990 until the air war, was a unique and bizarre
'first' in modern history. The holding of hundreds of foreign nationals
as hostages and the large numbers of people in hiding, which brought
processions of world leaders to Iraq in an effort to secure their release,
shed a quite new light on how civilians can be caught up in a war. The
way in which, despite differences of opinion, much of the world united
in its determination to force the invaders out of a small, peaceful and
defenceless country was up to that date unheard of. Financial
considerations certainly played a part in it, but so did other factors, and
the United Nations had never achieved anything like it before.

It was a modern type of warfare. This was the first time commanders
of the Coalition became public relations officers and conducted press
conferences and briefings live on television. It was fascinating to watch
them, but equally interesting to speculate on what was being left out.
On television the world was able to watch the spectacular bombing of
Baghdad as it took place. This meant that commanders did not conduct
operations wholly on military grounds, as in the past, but with an
awareness of the opinions of the general public; the 'mistaken'
bombing of the underground bunker in Baghdad illustrated that very

well. In the old manner of warfare no civilian would have been 'involved' until long after the event.

The dynamiting of hundreds of oil wells and opening of oil taps into the Gulf sea, the environmental damage this caused and its possible repercussions worldwide were other 'firsts', for havoc on such a scale had never been seen before. Many consider that there were grounds for prosecution in the actions of the leaders of Iraq; that their gross human rights record adds to their long list of criminal activities.

I should stress that the following account of the invasion records only a tiny part of the story. It would be impossible in one book to cover even half of what happened. Each person has a different and usually unpleasant tale to tell. The one pleasant part of the experience was the feeling of solidarity and closeness during the occupation. The people who were in Kuwait at that time now have an awareness and sympathy for those suffering similar experiences elsewhere. We all endured the war together and drew strength from that feeling.

Jehan S. Rajab
Kuwait
March 1993

PART I

Invasion
August 1990

1

The Scorpion Strikes

ON 1 August, my granddaughter's seventh birthday, my husband flew to Jordan for the weekend to visit the school we own there. The day before there had been a reception at the American Embassy to meet and welcome the new consul, Gail Rogers, and to say farewell to her predecessors, the Colwells, who were on the point of leaving Kuwait. The American ambassador, Nathaniel Howell, was also due to leave Kuwait at the end of his tenure there. Because the weather was hot, in fact searingly hot for those unused to living in this part of the world, many people were away on holiday. In short, amazing though it may seem and despite news from outside Kuwait, the atmosphere inside the country was calm and normal. If people thought about politics at all, and some did because they remembered Iraq's threat to invade in 1961, they only imagined noises on the border.

At 6.00 a.m. on 2 August I got out of bed as usual, opened the window and looked outside. To my consternation I heard the sharp staccato sounds of gunfire, not a shot or two but sustained firing, which was being answered back. The sounds resonated off the walls of the mosque beside us and it immediately and horrifyingly became obvious what was happening. Kuwait was being invaded by Iraq. I rapidly threw on some clothes and turned on the radio, which confirmed what I had assumed. As I tried to phone my daughter in England I could hear explosions coming from the down-town area of the city; the shooting still continued around us, though I was not exactly sure from where it originated. I also rang Jordan to try to reach my husband, but only managed to get a friend. I said in a quavering voice, 'Kuwait has been invaded by Iraq. Can you try and get hold of

Tareq and let him know we are all right,' to which the friend replied, 'No, no it's all right it won't happen.' It was quite hard to get him to understand that it had happened and we rang off in a state of shock. Another friend, who had rung a relative with the news, had been sharply reprimanded for telling silly jokes. It took some convincing for the dreadful truth to sink in and for people to realize that their lives had radically changed. Many lost their entire livelihoods, many died, or suffered imprisonment and torture, and the history of the Arab world, perhaps the whole world, took a new turn.

By early morning the American and British embassies were surrounded and, further down the road, fierce battles were being waged inside and outside the Amir's residence, the Dasman Palace. The Iraqis had headed straight for Sheikh Jaber Al Ahmad Al Sabah's palace, for they recognized the psychological and practical importance of capturing the Amir and forcing his surrender. By the end of that day the palace had been completely wrecked and looted, but fortunately the Amir had escaped. He had, with difficulty, been persuaded of the need to leave the country so that the government, of which he was the head, could continue in exile. The palace guards, as far as they had been able to against vastly superior numbers, had fought fiercely and many had lost their lives. We confronted a stark scene when we drove past the entrance to the palace a day or two later — burned-out cars, tanks and lorries on their sides and bits of twisted metal dug into the roundabouts. There were roadblocks everywhere and Iraqis standing about glowering and tight-lipped. It was obvious that the palace had been badly damaged inside as well as outside. When one of the residents of the palace compound had tried to get back in to see if he could rescue any of his possessions, he found all the houses torn apart, some burned out and people's belongings ripped and scattered all over the yard. He was stopped by soldiers but somehow managed to argue his way out. Had they realized that he had been a resident of the Dasman Palace, he would probably have been killed.

On that first day, Thursday, I went straight to our school, where many of the administrative staff were gathered around in small groups talking anxiously and phoning friends in various parts of the city to find out what was happening. Thursdays and Fridays are the weekend in this part of the world, but staff often come in to catch up on work in the morning. The New English School is a large one that caters to a

2

local and international student body from kindergarten through to Advanced-level examinations. Over the past 20 years its students, of many nationalities, have gone to virtually every important university in the Arab world, as well as in Britain and the USA. It was fortunately the summer holiday period, so there were few teachers or even students in Kuwait at that time. Most foreign and local people choose to take their holidays in August, the hottest month, in more temperate places, which the Iraqis must have realized and which probably influenced their timing of the invasion.

By the end of the first day of the invasion the Iraqis had cut all international telephone lines and we heard no more from the outside world for over seven months. However, most of the internal telephone lines remained working, which is surprising because an enormous amount of news was flashed around Kuwait by that means. Although rumours abounded, a great deal of what was passed on turned out to be remarkably accurate. It was especially surprising that the British and American embassies' local lines remained open. People rang up the embassies not only for information and help, but also to pass on anything that might be helpful and could be used against the Iraqis. In fact, practically all the arrangements between the British embassy, the people outside and the wardens were made over the telephone. Wardens are British people, usually of long-standing residence, whom the British consul appoints on an honorary basis to look after the interests and welfare of other British people in their area during periods of crisis. They, along with members of the embassy and Kuwaiti Resistance, helped work out details about hiding places for potential hostages, who included themselves, for wardens also had to go into hiding. This certainly made for some cryptic and interesting conversations, for it is probable that the lines were tapped almost immediately after the invasion. The Iraqis may have thought that if people told each other about the atrocities and killings that were taking place as the army invaded, everyone would quickly be frightened into subservience. No doubt they also thought that they might pick up information by listening to what people were saying. Because the lines were most likely tapped, everyone was very cautious about what they said and if they could speak a language other than Arabic, English or French they did.

3

It was common knowledge that a woman had been heard cursing Saddam Hussein to a friend on the telephone and that shortly after her conversation the dreaded *Mukhabarat* had turned up on her doorstep and shot her dead outside her house, leaving her body lying there for some time as a punishment and warning to other people. The *Mukhabarat* were the numerous and much-feared Iraqi secret police, known for their insane brutality. Gossip for many years insisted that certain branches were made up of orphans who had been trained in torture and rape and were accordingly without normal human emotions.

At school everyone was telephoning or being telephoned. The lines were constantly jangling and we were receiving news from all over the city and its environs. People in the main city area and near the Amir's palace were watching events from behind their curtains in frozen horror. A small boy standing on the balcony of his flat and clutching a small toy gun was shot at by the soldiers and nearly killed. Key installations, like Kuwait TV, had immediately been taken over, but the Kuwaiti radio station managed to go underground. It operated clandestinely for some days by moving from house to house and keeping just one step ahead of the Iraqis. It broadcasted up-to-date news about the invasion, exhorted the Kuwaitis to keep resisting the Iraqis and informed us that, according to Baghdad, a revolution, or *thawra*, had overthrown the Kuwaiti government — a story the Iraqis had to drop very quickly as they could not find enough, if any, Kuwaitis to support it. Desperately *Hona el Kuwait* (This is Kuwait) appealed to the world and other Arab countries for help. It continued to try to operate within Kuwait but the Iraqis were closing in and it had to retreat deep into the desert: it eventually set up the Free Kuwait Radio Station from Saudi Arabia.

At school all thoughts of work were abandoned. People stood around in small groups in the school yard nervously discussing the situation and exchanging tales they had been told by friends in other parts of town. A deep droning sound impinged on our consciousness and large numbers of helicopter gunships began to fly low over the school looking very menacing. They were heading for the city centre and must have been landing more soldiers along the seafront. Everyone rushed out to look at them and it reminded me of an incident in Brighton (England) many years earlier at the beginning of the Second

4

World War, when a German warplane had flown low down through the main street hotly pursued by a Spitfire. The crowds out shopping had stopped in their tracks to watch the dogfight taking place above them, which ended with the German plane being shot down and dropping into the sea. No one had been alarmed at that point, just interested and curious. Later on, however, people came to realize that it was dangerous to watch such things and would scatter and run for shelter.

Shooting continued in sporadic bursts and, later in the morning, Iraqi tanks and personnel carriers, with soldiers in full battle fatigues, came round in small convoys. We stared at them in amazement and horror and they glared back haughtily. Occasionally a truck or car filled with Filipinos would pass by, for their embassy was not far away, giving an impression of a disturbed ants nest in a panic. One bus had a hastily scrawled notice along its sides reading 'Filipino Contract Workers — Peace — No Violence'. Even on that first day many civilians had already been shot at and molested.

Amongst the calls to school came the news that Sheikh Fahed, a younger brother of the Amir, had been killed in the fighting at the Dasman Palace. This striking-looking, somewhat flamboyant sheikh had fought against and been wounded and captured by the Israelis while with the Palestinians in the Lebanon. He had also been president of the Kuwait Olympic Committee and held other sports titles. Months later some of the people who managed, with great difficulty, to get into the palace grounds, surreptitiously remove his body and conceal it in the Amiri Hospital mortuary revealed the truth about his death and subsequent burial. Iraqi undercover police had frequently visited the hospital to try and find out if Sheikh Fahed's body was there and mortuary workers told harrowing tales of their efforts to keep the body hidden.

A rumour circulating early on in the invasion and substantiated after the liberation by official government and newspaper reports was that Oddai, Saddam's son, had wanted Sheikh Fahed's head brought to him in Baghdad. Accordingly his body had to remain nameless for some time before it could receive any sort of burial. Throughout the occupation a Kuwaiti, Waled Al Fadel, acted as coordinator between the Kuwait Red Crescent Society and the cemeteries. One day he received a mysterious telephone call from his friend, Ali Al Zomai, a

Resistance leader, asking him to come quickly to the Amiri Hospital. There they learned that it was now a matter of urgency to try and bury Sheikh Fahed before the Iraqi authorities realized that his body was lying in the mortuary. Not only had it been refrigerated in difficult circumstances for some time, but the Iraqis were still more than anxious to locate it. Indeed, according to the grapevine, the Iraqi Army officer in charge of delivering the head to Baghdad had himself been 'removed' for failing to do so.

Sheikh Fahed's body was hurriedly taken out to a waiting ambulance, along with that of a young Egyptian who had been tortured to death by the Iraqis. Despite trying to avoid the frequent Iraqi road check posts *en route* to the cemetery, the party ran straight into one. But the spokesman calmly told the soldiers that the two bodies inside the ambulance were unidentified and that, because refrigeration facilities in the hospital were now overflowing, they had to dispose of some to make room for others. After a cursory glance into the ambulance the party was allowed to continue. The burial took place without a ceremony and the name 'Abdullah Al Masri' was hastily written over the grave. 'Abdullah' because that means 'the servant of God' and Al Masri, 'the Egyptian', because Sheikh Fahed was buried near the unknown Egyptian who had also been killed by the Iraqis.

Some time later we heard about a Kuwaiti family living near the official government guesthouse. This section of the town stood right in the path of the advancing Iraqi Army and when the lady of the house had got out of bed early that morning and looked out of her window, she had seen armed soldiers standing around in her front garden. Puzzled as to why the Kuwait Army, as she first thought, should be there, she woke her husband who went to investigate. As he reached the dining area at the back of their house, which had a large glass window looking onto the garden, a man crashed through into the room. He was a Kuwaiti who had run into the advancing army while driving to work. The soldiers had tried to capture him, but he had flung open his car door, tumbled out and run away. In his attempt to evade them, he had climbed up and over a wall into their garden and come crashing through the dining room window. Although cut and bleeding from the glass he was helped to his feet and quickly hidden.

The other Kuwaiti went out to the soldiers in his garden to learn that his country had been taken over by the Iraqis.

Because a number of main roads converge at a large roundabout on the outskirts of the city centre, many people on their way to work had similar experiences in the government guesthouse area. Cars and vans were stopped by army jeeps and tanks and their occupants ordered (or dragged) out — Kuwaitis can be extremely argumentative. Some were pushed roughly into waiting lorries and then transported, in the searing heat and without water, to gaols all over Iraq. A few were released within days, others much later on, and there were some who never returned. Other Kuwaitis and foreigners were made to stand or sit on the ground with their hands over their heads, while their vehicles were taken away or looted. Eventually the soldiers shot into the crowds to disperse people, killing a number and leaving the rest to walk home as best they could. It is a sobering thought that most civilians in Kuwait knew little about the invasion until they actually ran into it themselves.

Along the seafront towards the centre of town, there was fighting near the Seif Palace, which was where the Amir and his government worked and received official visitors. The old section, an ochre-coloured building, had been described in 1912 by the Danish author and traveller B. Raunkiaer as a 'burnt yellow brick two-storey building'. It had two audience halls and a gallery with windows inset with panes of coloured glass 'through which the sun could filter its softened rays'. A newer section of the complex is a pleasant rather North African-looking clock tower, which had been built over 30 years ago. Alongside that stands a very new structure which attempts to appear Arab and Islamic, but does not quite achieve that aim, although it is pleasant enough. During the last days of the occupation the entire Seif Palace complex was spitefully torn apart, its pillars broken, furniture wrecked, papers and books destroyed and vandalized and then as much as possible set on fire by the retreating Iraqis.

A former pupil, who was now a goldsmith, rang to say that the gold shops in the souk in the old part of town were being broken into and that the jewellery was disappearing into the pockets of eager soldiers. This was followed by numerous stories of dead soldiers being found wearing a pair or two of heavy gold anklets under their trousers and with their pockets stuffed with rings and necklaces. Shortly after the invasion many Iraqi women took to coming into Kuwait to join the 'unofficial' looting of shops in the marketplace. Official looting consisted of emptying and then vandalizing institutes, government schools, the university, the houses of important government employees and the homes of members of the Al Sabah family. It was carried out openly and under direct orders from Baghdad, with soldiers filling large army lorries or juggernauts with every item of equipment and furniture in the building and then transporting them to Iraq to be distributed 'more fairly in the other provinces'. One friend, the daughter of an important government officer, actually saw her house being emptied one morning as she drove slowly past the building. Made-up beds were being manhandled through the bedroom windows and thrown on top of the already piled-up lorry. Shopping complexes often seemed to fall into the category of 'official'. Only one escaped lightly, despite the merchants packing up and hiding their goods and shutting up their shops. It was widely believed that Saddam's son, Oddai, 'wanted' the shopping complex and stock market building. Though the Iraqi government denied it was happening, unofficial looting was a free-for-all that went on day and night from the moment the soldiers entered Kuwait until the day they left. It was medieval in its intensity and, although in theory forbidden, the Baghdad authorities allowed and obviously encouraged it.

Bank employees rang the school to intimate cautiously that attempts were being made to empty the Central Bank of its bullion. If safe combinations could not be obtained, and people went into hiding to avoid giving that information, then the safes were blown open. The school safe, which was a tough little one but very heavy, was eventually split apart with a thick iron bar and it ended up looking like a peeled back sardine tin. There was in fact nothing in it, for everything had been removed before the army reached the school. Had the soldiers bothered to check, they would have seen that it had even been unlocked.

On the first afternoon we took down the name on the wall over the Tareq Rajab Museum and, along with our neighbours, rushed around pulling off street signs and hiding them. With a view to confusing and holding up the enemy's search for key people, most house owners had had their names either blocked in or removed from their front doors. The family name over our door, a raised one on a brass plate, proved impossible to prise out. After some thought and keeping a close watch on the road for the army jeeps on constant patrol, a wodge of Plasticine was spread carefully over the brass and then coloured with a fingerful of paint to complete the operation. Although the Iraqis must have had maps, not to mention many informants who already knew their way around, Kuwait is a confusing place in which to find residences and taking down those signs hopefully added to the army's problems. Even though it was now hot in the evenings as well during the day, when I went to bed that night I left my window open just a little in order to be able to hear if anything happened. The window remained that way until well after the liberation. It is still hard to keep it completely closed even in the very hot, dusty or cold weather.

2

Kuwaiti Women Demonstrate

THE first few days following the invasion were very confusing because nobody could take in the enormity and horror of what was happening to a normally safe and secure Kuwait. People had not yet quite understood exactly what kind of regime they were up against. The eight-year Iraq–Iran war had obviously posed dangers to Kuwait and it had certainly been possible for the fighting to spill over the border. There had been occasions, especially towards the end, when the actual sounds of battle could be heard and felt in the not so far away distance. In the house in which we then lived, the large glass windows leading onto the garden had on a couple of occasions rattled and shaken violently for days on end to explosions as the combatants battled back and forth in the Shatt al Arab area.

An attempt on the Amir's life had nearly succeeded when a car packed with explosives had tried to ram his car while he was on the way to work. There were a number of other violent efforts to blow up various installations. One such attempt at the Ministry of Electricity's main office had been foiled by a guard who firmly refused, despite arguments, to let a man pass without the correct papers. The man and his associates had been planning to lay charges in strategic places and blow up the building. As it was the main electricity station, considerable problems would have been caused had the plan succeeded. Oddly enough that main centre survived the Iraqis as well; although its rooms were ripped and torn apart the building itself remained standing and relatively undamaged. During the last part of the occupation the electricity all over Kuwait gradually shut down, first the street lighting, then the houses, until nothing was left. Only the red warning light at the top of the building still glowed in the evening and was something of a source of comfort to those who could see it.

In 1983 a series of explosions had ripped through the American and French embassies. The school, which is only a short distance from the French buildings, was violently shaken and one or two windows in the chemistry laboratories had cracked down their length. A fire drill had satisfactorily emptied the school in a calm, orderly manner, with all 2,300 pupils pouring outside in two minutes. Parents rushed into the school in an understandable panic when a rumour flashed around that the building had been hit — an official computer reading mistakenly saying that explosions had taken place 'in' instead of 'near' the New English School. Obviously conditions were unstable, but so were they elsewhere, and everyone learned to live with and understand why these events were taking place. No one seriously believed, probably because they did not want to, that Kuwait could actually become embroiled, least of all invaded, for throughout its history the country had always remained free and independent.

Many people were dismayed when Iraq instigated the war against Iran. Naive though it may now seem, however, the average person in Kuwait then believed that 'Arab brothers' should stand by one another. Irrespective of whether the government adopted this somewhat injudicious stance, most people had been in favour of the help and money that both private individuals and public bodies had given to aid Iraq. It was thus a bitter experience for Kuwait — and the subject was constantly discussed throughout the occupation — that some of the Arab countries that had been given so much financial and other help over so many years had supported Iraq's invasion of Kuwait. It is a pleasure to be able to record, however, that the United Arab Emirates showed their appreciation for past assistance by offering help and sympathy to Kuwaiti refugees during the occupation.

Reports of atrocities began to circulate within the first 10 days of the invasion. Filipina women had been lined up and raped, two young Kuwaiti women trying to run away from some soldiers had been shot down in cold blood, and a German woman had been caught in her flat and assaulted. One of my friends had been horrified on opening her curtains one morning to see two bullet-punctured bleeding bodies dangling over the compound walls, the smell of death already strong in the hot morning sunshine. They were beyond help and no one was allowed to touch or remove them until permission had been given by the authorities. On the first day of the invasion and still unaware that Kuwait had been attacked, that same friend's brother was out early delivering food supplies to the Amir's residence, the Dasman Palace. As he approached the roundabout and began to turn towards the gates he realized, too late, what was happening and was dragged out of his van and severely beaten by the soldiers. Pulling himself up off the ground and lucky to escape with his life, he staggered home on foot in a terrible state of shock and pain. A few days later he risked returning to see if he could rescue his van, for it was a large valuable one. He found it there relatively intact, but only because it contained a large amount of what had then been fresh meat. In that blistering heat the van was nearly impossible to approach because of the smell but, holding a towel to his nose, he was able to get in and drive it away. Somehow the van managed to outlast the occupation although, to this day, in spite of much washing and scrubbing, the faint smell of decay still lingers.

Every day the stunned population either heard about or witnessed new acts of violence. There had been some kind of battle or massacre in the Kaifan Gardens, after which the dying and dead bodies of Kuwaitis and Indians had lain in the burning sun for some days. The cooperatives and few supermarkets that had remained open were quickly crowded out with people panic buying supplies. It suddenly became apparent how much Kuwaiti eating habits had changed over the past 20 years. Tins of baby milk, Pampers (baby nappies), hamburgers and Pepsi became very important items to try and obtain, followed by staples like tea, sugar, flour, rice and cooking oil. People under the age of about 30 hankered for fizzy drinks, which along with everything else became hard to get and finally disappeared altogether.

Stories percolated through of Americans and other westerners who had begun to try and escape by driving across the desert into Saudi Arabia. Like others, one school parent failed in his first attempt, but had driven back to his flat determined to try again. Bill and his wife, a junior school teacher, reported that Iraqi soldiers had swarmed into the Shuaiba Port, where he worked, smashed many of the computers in the port in the mistaken belief that they were televisions that did not work, and were in the process of taking 3000 fully loaded containers to Iraq. Long lines of tanks, guns and men rolled along the expressways and roadblocks began to appear everywhere, even on minor and unimportant roads. Everyone desperately wanted to believe that the Iraqis would take what they could and then pull back out of Kuwait. There would still be time to prepare for the opening of school and we would return — almost — to our normal lives. Although gossip and even common sense had begun to suggest less pleasant alternatives, it was still hard to believe that the Iraqis intended to stay.

On 5 August there was a sudden loud explosion, which came from down the expressway not far from the school and our house. A ball of fire followed by clouds of black smoke soon revealed that the large Central Intelligence Department building was on fire. Fire engines eventually drove up, deliberately late as always, but the building rapidly became a blackened wreck. Above the roar of the flames were occasional small booms as the fire burned its way through wire and fitments. And above that were added the jagged sounds of intermittent shooting, for many Kuwaitis lived in the houses of that particular area and they put up continued resistance during the long months that followed.

Within the first week of the invasion Kuwaiti women decided to demonstrate on the streets against what had happened. For a short period it was as if the whole of Kuwait held its breath in confusion, shock and open-mouthed disbelief. Then the women, always direct in their attitudes, prepared to show publicly their complete non-acceptance of the invasion and the violence that had gone with it. With banners and flags, sometimes joined by other nationalities and many dressed for solidarity in their black *abat* (mantles), the women of different districts organized themselves and walked out solidly in protest.

As I stood watching the road from my kitchen window, a string of army jeeps swept by filled with armed Republican Guards — the Red Berets, or professional soldiers of the Iraqi Army. Suddenly the telephone rang shrilly and I picked it up, still watching the armed men in the jeeps. It was a friend saying that demonstrations were taking place just down the road in Jabriya if I wanted to go and join them. Slamming down the phone I rushed to my cupboard to look for some kind of head scarf, as much because of the heat and need, even in the late afternoon, to shield myself from the sun as because many women were also wearing *abat* as a sign of solidarity. After a brief stop down the road to collect my husband's niece, Rowa, she and I ran straight to where we had heard the demonstrators would be gathering.

Many people were standing in the middle of the road, some men, but mostly women with their teenage daughters and younger children, who were clutching spray cans in their hands. There was a feeling of tension and expectancy: it was almost as if the crowd subconsciously realized that even peaceful demonstrations would not be countenanced by the Iraqis. There were perhaps 300 people there, with others like ourselves arriving or being dropped off by car. The organizers handed out banners, posters of the Amir and Crown Prince and paper and cloth Kuwaiti flags of all sizes. We all took a flag, banner or poster and held it up proudly, feeling that at last there was an opportunity to show plainly what the whole of Kuwait felt.

At 5.00 p.m. on the first Tuesday after the invasion, when the heat of the sun became a little less ferocious, though by most standards it was still very hot, the crowd began to move off, walking slowly down the centre of the street waving banners and shouting slogans such as *'Allah-u-Akbar'* (God is Great), 'Long Live Kuwait' and *'Aish Jaber'* (Long Live the Amir), interspersed rather unnervingly with 'Death to Saddam' and 'Saddam is a Zionist'. Doors opened all along the road, old and young poured out of their houses and some quickly ran to join the demonstrators. Others cheered and clapped as the crowd passed by. The Pakistanis, Indians and Filipinos who were standing watching also cheered and clapped, while young boys and girls rushed out of their houses with bottles of cold water to slake the thirsts of the demonstrators. People poured with sweat and their throats grew dry from shouting. It is hard work demonstrating in such heat. I noticed that soldiers going past in their jeeps looked stunned and disbelieving, which as will be seen was not surprising. When dusk fell after about two hours of going up and down as many streets as possible, we returned to our starting point, where we were told to come back again at the same time the next day to demonstrate once more.

Because the news had spread there were even more people present at the same meeting point on the following day (Wednesday 7th) and similar demonstrations were apparently taking place in all areas in which large numbers of Kuwaitis lived. Once more waving their flags and banners and shouting slogans as loudly as they could, the demonstrators marched past the Chinese and French embassies, stopping for

15

a while to ensure that the people inside realized that it was an anti-Iraqi demonstration. On turning down a road the marchers began to proceed past the three big schools, including ours, where children were spraying graffiti ('Death to Saddam') along the walls. I felt quite proud that worthwhile slogans such as 'Long Live Kuwait' and 'Long live the Amir' were being scribbled on those walls, but later realized that these children had been dicing with death. Had they been caught, as some were in Failaka Island and elsewhere in Kuwait, they risked being beaten up and even taken home and shot in front of their parents. An engineer I knew who had been based in Failaka insisted that five young boys caught in the act of pining up posters had been grabbed by the Iraqis, scalped and then shot.

A small incident occurred as the crowd snaked past the walls of the Iranian school. The road was narrow with a parallel fence that gave onto the main Fahaheel Expressway. Parked on the other side of the fence was a broken-down tank with seven Iraqi soldiers, one of them half under the tank and trying to repair it. The women walked by loudly chanting their slogans, the young boys were busy spraying anti-Saddam graffiti all along the walls. Suddenly, like a flock of birds that wheel in the sky simultaneously, the women turned and faced the tank and shouted 'Long Live Kuwait, Death to Saddam' and 'Long live Jaber' (the Amir). Being of a fairly practical turn of mind it occurred to me then that if the soldiers decided to shoot we were trapped, for there was nowhere much to run; we were backed up against a long wall and the road we were on was hemmed in by the fence for quite some way. I involuntarily shrank back against the wall but continued to wave my flag and shout the slogans. One soldier rattled his Kalashnikov rifle, did the thumbs down sign and grinned nastily; the other five firmly ignored us and looked the other way until, having stressed their point, the women turned forward once more and continued round the corner and on down the road.

The third demonstration the next afternoon set off as usual at around 5.00 p.m. with even more people present. Each day the organizers led us on a different route, no doubt to cover as much of the district as possible. Once again men, women and children came out of their houses to cheer, while some ran quickly across to join the procession. On this occasion cars that had been driving by continued to move slowly alongside the crowd and the whole event began to take on the atmosphere of a triumphant football match celebration. (Being a car-loving country, winning important matches is regarded by Kuwaiti enthusiasts as an opportunity to drive through the streets cheering and energetically waving flags.) Perhaps a bit ominously, even an ambulance was following us at the rear. After some twists and turns into side streets we began to walk up the long wide main avenue that would lead the crowd past the Jabriya police station. The station had been taken over after a fight on 2 August by the Iraqi Army and was partially burned out. With the Iraqis in the station were quite a number of armed Palestinians, who may have belonged to the Abu Nidal group reputed to have come down from Baghdad with the army.

By now cars were driving on both sides of the road, the women were moving up the centre of the island and chanting '*La-illaha-illa-allah*' (There is no God but God), flags were waving and car horns were tooting. People still came running out of their houses to offer welcome bottles of cold water and some stayed to join the women. At the front there was also a Kuwaiti walking backwards filming the demonstration, a dangerous action for which, even at that early date, death was the penalty. One young woman, Samira, was later caught trying to photograph scenes of devastation in Kuwait and was arrested. As far as I know she has not been heard of since; only one message came to her family from a released prisoner of war who thought he saw her in a Baghdad prison, blinded and with her head shaven.

About 150 yards down the road from the police station an organizer stopped us and spoke quietly to the crowd. He suggested that it might be politic when we trooped past the station not to chant provocative slogans like 'Death to Saddam', but just to keep to '*Allah-u-Akbar*'. The crowd drew in its breath and seemed to move collectively backwards for a moment, as if it had some premonition of what was going to happen; then, banners waving defiantly, everyone firmly stepped forward chanting loudly '*Allah-u-Akbar*'.

A couple of minutes later the armed men at the police station fired straight down into the crowd. Pandemonium broke out. Car engines roared as they tried to back wildly down the road, people screamed and the shooting continued. My niece threw herself down 'behind' the smallest, flattest little bush that ever grew. I remained standing, staring back at a young man some feet away who was lying on his back with his face a pale deathly grey. Rowa bawled at me, 'Hit the

17

dust, Jehan,' and, just before I did so, I saw the yellow flash of bullets to my left at chest level. The palm tree I tried to fit myself round was a skimpy little thing and I remember thinking that if a bullet hit me and, astonishingly, I could imagine the sharp sting as it entered my skin, the tree would give very little protection. At a lower level of consciousness I was amazed that the mind could bother about all these things at such a moment. This probably all took only a few minutes, but it seemed much longer. When there was a break in the shooting I struggled up off the ground to find that Rowa had gone and that people were running in all directions. I hoped she was all right and wondered what my sister-in-law would say to me if she had been hurt or killed. I looked behind to the young man in black still lying on the ground groaning slightly and headed for him to see what, if anything, could be done. As I reached him three of his women relatives ran across from the other side of the road, picked him up bodily, carried him to where a reversing car had stopped and somehow pushed him into the back seat. I believe that this poor young man had been hit by bullets and died later in the hospital.

There was an awful thought that the army might chase the crowd by jeep and possibly even on foot, so, having watched the young man pushed into a reversing car, I dashed over the road fully intending to try and dig myself into a nearby sandhill that had been dumped outside a house. All the doors were unlatched and people were taking refuge inside. As I ran up someone indicated that I should step in. Suddenly a completely hysterical woman, her black *abaya* and head wraps streaming out behind her came tearing around the corner screaming, 'They've killed her, they shot her, she's dead, she's dead.' The women tried to calm her down and get her to tell them what had happened, but she continued to weep hysterically at the shock of what she had seen.

At that moment renewed shooting from the police station broke out and I decided instead to run home through the side streets as fast as I could. All the way along I was stopped by men and women crowding outside their doors who wanted to know what had happened, for they could clearly hear the outbursts of shooting. Puffing and panting and red in the face with heat, excitement and unaccustomed exertion, I told them about how the soldiers had fired straight into the crowd of unarmed women and children and possibly killed or injured some. As

I was once more relating the story to a man on the pavement, a car screeched round the corner on two wheels, both the driver and the man beside him with their arms out of the windows holding large guns. For a split second I thought that they were Iraqis in hot pursuit and that this time we were dead. The car jolted to a halt beside us and one of them demanded to know what had happened. They were in fact Kuwaitis and, possibly, were (or were to become) part of the Resistance. Organized Resistance fighters were operating within a couple of weeks of the invasion, but people had become active individually in some form or another almost from the first day. Police checkpoints were a particularly popular target and were frequently blown up after dark. In fact the bodies of soldiers were regularly found in the early mornings down the road from the school near a turning onto the expressway. From the mosques came secret news-sheets and information on first aid and what to do if a chemical attack took place.

The men in the car tore off in the direction of the police station, presumably to try and fight the Iraqis and Palestinians there. Certainly the sounds of gunfire could be heard for quite some time afterwards. As I continued on my way, always watching the road cautiously, one person who had listened to my story gently said, 'I think you should fold up the flag you are carrying. It might be dangerous if you are caught with it.' I had clutched that flag throughout all the demonstrations and now I folded it round its handle. But I was unable to put it away because my hand was wrapped so tightly round the stick that it was impossible to release it. That flag somehow symbolized Kuwait and its determination to remain an independent country.

That was the last of such marches in our district, and probably the last anywhere, for the Iraqis shot to kill or maim. In another area a woman had lost a leg from gunshot wounds in a similar incident. Kuwaitis were beginning to understand just how ruthless the invaders were. There had been a tradition in this part of the Arab world, which to some extent still prevailed, that women and children were sacrosanct and could not be touched or killed. It originated amongst the Bedouin tribes and, although beginning to break down in the twentieth century, still existed, at least in the Gulf. The shooting of unarmed women and children was yet another sign of what Kuwait could expect.

My niece had been given a lift home by someone who had seen her running down the road, for she too had thought that the crowd might be chased. She had noticed a woman with a badly bleeding leg being helped into a car nearby. Another young woman, Sena Al Foudry, who had been at the head of the demonstration with her female relatives, had been killed; others had been wounded. Although hit by a bullet, Sena Al Foudry, a university chemistry student, had insisted on remaining where she was and on continuing to hold up her banner and demonstrate. When it was eventually recovered, her body had been pumped full of bullet holes. As we later realized, the regime seemed to have been obsessed with shooting dead bodies: the soldiers would walk past grinning and emptying cartridges into them. Sena Al Foudry became one of the first *shehid* (martyrs) to die for her country. After the liberation a new street sign went up on the road on which she had lived — 'The street of the Martyr Sena Al Foudry'. This was placed there by the residents of the road and in due course will no doubt be acknowledged by the Kuwait municipality, which intends to name previously numbered roads, such as that street.

3

Looting, Pillage, Rape and Resistance

ON the Friday two weeks after the invasion the mosque opposite our house, which had always been well attended, was packed with people, their cars lining the street and the wasteland nearby. When he came to give his sermon, the mullah (preacher) spoke out loudly against the invasion, saying that it did not seem to be the correct way of solving any problems. The megaphone remains on during the sermon and this time loud voices from the congregation were raised in the middle of what he was saying. Arguments broke out and the sermon came to an abrupt, acrimonious end, with prayers finishing rapidly. The *Mukhabarat* attended Friday prayers here as everywhere and had not allowed him to continue. I do not know what happened to that particular mullah, whether he was arrested or managed to escape, but I did not see him again. Instead the men living in the houses around us took turns to conduct the five daily prayers. Elsewhere the occupation authorities forced the preachers to praise the *jihad* (holy war) and, rather than have to repeat such lies, many of the mosque staff went into hiding.

After that incident I watched the mosque closely, especially during Friday prayers, but although the army were by then occupying a government school nearby, our school and the Iranian school further down the road, only once did I see three soldiers attend prayers. It was easy to pick out the *Mukhabarat* — with their generally dowdy suits, Saddam moustaches and grim, cold eyes they were unmistakable. The mosque was a comfort because throughout those grey and dangerous days one knew they were a focus for resistance. In spite of a dusk-to-

21

dawn curfew, people somehow continued to attend the night and early-morning prayers. There was a feeling that we were all in it together. The distribution of food, so long as there was any food to distribute, took place from the mosque, which was when I first realized how important fizzy drinks were to the younger members of the population. News-sheets secretly printed by the Resistance were distributed to the populace through the mosques. Even during the air war, when Kuwait was shaking and rattling from the bombing, one of the men would walk over to the mosque at the correct time and give the call to prayer in a calm orderly manner, which so impressed me that I once ran up to the roof and managed to tape the call alongside the shooting and the explosion of bombs.

The exodus of frightened refugees fleeing for their lives had begun on the first day of the invasion. News of shootings, rapes and other barbarities was quickly broadcast around Kuwait over the telephones. Because the army was allowed to raid the central stores, food shortages became apparent and, in protest and out of necessity, the merchants closed their doors. Kuwait is in the vulnerable position of possessing little food or water of its own. The climate is severe, with intense heat during the summer and cold periods during the short winter season. With a rising population, distillation plants using sea water had long replaced the water wells and electricity substations kept the water running and the houses cooled. The prospect of dying of hunger, or worse, of thirst, seemed a grim possibility and further encouraged the flow of refugees out of Kuwait.

By 20 August Iraq had ordered all foreign embassies to shut down and relocate to Baghdad. But 25 of them, including the Americans and British, refused to close and their buildings were immediately surrounded by armed soldiers and tanks. Ambassadors and their staff became prisoners in their compounds, cut off from supplies of food, water and even electricity. One ambassador whose electricity cables had been disconnected managed to connect one to the next-door house to keep their refrigerator working. Under cover of darkness he and a colleague had climbed over the wall and had even obtained a small supply of water from a carefully concealed hose. With such chaotic conditions prevailing, westerners were advised by their embassies to keep their heads down and, as far as possible, to avoid going outside.

Other ambassadors to Kuwait, including the Canadian, Turkish, Japanese and Bulgarian, were away on leave at the time of the invasion. On hearing the news, they immediately attempted to fly, or drive, back to their posts in Kuwait. But they were rebuffed by the Iraqi authorities and the closest they could get was to Amman in Jordan. When the ambassadors informed the Iraqis that they wished to return to their embassies in Kuwait, they met blank looks and were sternly asked if 'they meant the nineteenth province'. Just as sternly the ambassadors replied that they meant the State of Kuwait. They tried by every means possible to get over the border and back into their residences, but were firmly prevented from doing so.

Mr Douglas Croskery was a British citizen working in Kuwait who decided, as did so many others, to attempt to escape in his car across the sands. He was shot dead on 11 August by Iraqi troops in the desert somewhere near the Saudi border in unexplained circumstances. Larry Banks, the British consul, made three journeys from the beleaguered embassy under an Iraqi Army escort to try and recover his body. It has never been found. A rumour percolated through our telephone network that he had been shot while trying to help people who were stuck in the sand, but we had no means of knowing the truth about that tragic event. In addition to westerners trying to leave, many of the residents of Jahra and Sulaibikhat fled into the desert, for both localities are situated near the head of the Bay of Kuwait and were in the path of the army as it poured in through the desert from Basra. People awoke to shooting and the heavy rumble of tanks along their streets. Soldiers entered many private houses, where they stole money and jewellery, raped the women and demanded food and drink. Dozens, many still in their nightclothes and clutching their children, had tried to get across the border into Saudi Arabia. Some suffered dehydration when their cars got stuck in the sand and they tried to dig them out, some were shot at by Iraqis and others lost their lives driving through the burning desert.

Some of the Egyptian cleaners from our school told us that one of their group in the town had, along with many others, been forced into a bus and driven to Hawalli. This district, which had been in the desert 40 years earlier, was known for its fresh-water wells, which are so vital in arid parts of the world. It had been inhabited by a small settlement of Kuwaitis who grew tomatoes for the local market. Over the years it gradually became a thriving township of government schools, flats, shops and villas and was now inhabited mainly by Palestinians. Some had arrived in the 1930s as skilled personnel in the teaching and administrative professions, but the majority of the 400,000 now living in Kuwait had come as refugees after the 1967 and 1973 wars with Israel. Kuwait had given them refuge on both occasions and all schools, private and public, had been told to do all they could to assist them.

The Egyptians said that the bus had stopped in a wide street and the men been ordered out and told to demonstrate and shout 'Long Live Saddam'-type slogans. Though reluctant, they had to comply, for they were being photographed for local and Iraqi TV consumption to show how happy everyone in Kuwait was at what had happened. Our cleaner, an inoffensive and by now completely dazed man, had been clapping his hands in a lack-lustre fashion when suddenly the butt of a rifle hit him hard in the ribs. He was ordered to put some 'pep' into his demonstration or it would be the worse for him. With the army standing by ready to deal with anyone who lacked suitable enthusiasm, he naturally obliged in a frenzied manner. The film was shown on Kuwaiti television a couple of times. Like most Iraqi propaganda films it was obvious that these 'shows' had been filmed in a restricted area with the camera zooming back and forth to take pictures of the same people from different angles. Since Kuwait is a comparatively small place it was easy to see where it had been filmed. Had the shots been taken anywhere else there would have been a high risk of sniper attacks. From the manner of their dress it was quite obvious that the 'Kuwaitis' in the film were Iraqis and that most other nationalities had, as far as possible, tried to melt into the background to avoid being made to participate in such an absurd situation.

Accompanying that film on TV was a short feature about the Sultan Centre Supermarket, which stocked just about anything one could want. Run on very modern lines and with a magnificent fruit and vegetable section, it had apparently been quite famous in Iraq for selling seven 'different colours of peppers'. Lined up on a shelf the capsicums did look rather splendid — red, yellow, green, white, purple, orange and black — all shiny and glistening. Near them were tomatoes, lettuces, cauliflower and a good range of other vegetables. Our overseas visitors had sometimes taken photographs of these splendid displays. Within the first few days of the invasion, however, all commodities were considerably depleted, for everyone had been out panic buying and the supply system had come to a complete stop.

The film that was shown that evening and for a few days afterwards featured a colourful display of fruit and vegetables in a supermarket packed with cheerful shoppers that no longer existed. The camera then shifted its focus over to a somewhat smarmy man placing his purchases in his car and getting into the driving seat. Leaning over to his opposite side window just before he moved off into the traffic, one saw him smiling and saying in a relaxed manner, 'It's absolutely marvellous here and I can get everything I want.' The true situation by then was quite the opposite, there had been rush buying and no one looked or felt relaxed and happy, for there was no longer much left to purchase and, more importantly, people did not have that amount of ready money. Over the next seven months the Sultan Centre in fact secretly distributed a considerable amount of financial aid to distressed Kuwaiti families. Interestingly, the film must have been made at least two weeks, if not longer, before the invasion, which seemed to suggest that the Iraqis had not invaded on the spur of the moment.

Ten days into the occupation few of the administrative staff at school were able to come in because there were so many inspections and searches along every road. The soldiers would swoop down on side streets and block them off, their eyes swiftly picking out suitable cars to remove from their owners. From the first day of the invasion the Iraqis lusted after the many different types of vehicles in Kuwait, with BMWs and Mercedes popular with top officials and four-wheel-drives with everyone. Within two weeks of the invasion cars — indeed anything with wheels — were being stolen outright, but various other ploys were also used to part people from their cars. As Saddam Hussein later replied to a journalist's question about the prevalence of looting in Kuwait: 'It was lies about theft of any sort taking place in the 19th Province. There were laws against such actions.' This was no doubt quite true, but what happened was that the laws were interpreted to suit the Iraqis with the full connivance of their highest authority.

A popular method of removing a car from its owner was to stop it at an inspection point and ask the driver to produce his or her ID and the blue book every car carries. If the name on the car book did not match the driver's ID that person was immediately accused of stealing it and taken off to a police station, where he or she was then likely to be charged with theft. One Kuwaiti, who was driving his wife's car about 100 yards from his house, was stopped by soldiers in a sudden snap inspection along the road. He was ordered to return to his house on foot and to bring back the papers proving that the car belonged to his wife and that his wife was his wife. He hurried down the road and returned with the papers, only to find that both the soldiers and the car had disappeared. He never found it again, as the police stations had 'no knowledge of it'. Without the 'right' papers one risked being tried, gaoled, or even put to death for being a thief. Towards the end of the occupation cars were simply stolen outright without any pretence of the law being applied. I had to give up driving altogether because my car was in my husband's name and he was not even in the country. In any case, being a Nissan Safari, the car was on the very popular list and so, like many other vehicles, it had to go into hiding.

A young Indian, whose parents were on holiday, always used their car to drive to church services in town. But one Sunday, just before reaching the church, he ran into a roadblock. After showing his licence and the car book, he was asked to explain why the car was not in his name. He was then arrested and gaoled in Kuwait for the next two months. The church authorities tried to vouch for him and hired a lawyer for his defence. Suddenly he was sent for 'trial' to Basra where, though understanding very little of what was going on, he was acquitted. Instead of being released, however, he was transported to the prison in Diwaniya, another town in Iraq. Somehow he managed to smuggle a pathetic letter to Kuwait, in which he wrote that there was very little food and that people were squashed together in a small room in sordid circumstances. They were being beaten and worse and he did not expect to survive. But his story had a happy ending. When Diwaniya was bombed during the air war, the opposition opened the prison gates and released all the inmates. And, as did so many other people, he managed to get back to Kuwait, walking most of the way.

By the middle of August a steady stream of soldiers, who were always armed, began walking and driving past the school. Their sharp eyes darted about, noting everything, and they used various pretexts to come in and ask about any vehicles they could see. It seemed better to try and remove from public view some of the staff cars which, along with 60 buses, were parked for the summer in the school yard. When dusk had fallen, my son, Nadr, and colleague, Abu Ali, drove the cars over to my older son's house next door to mine. As each car appeared, and watching carefully in case a jeep or lorry went by, I opened the gates. The two passages on either side of the house were able to hold eight cars, which were then covered and parked one behind the other to make it as difficult as possible to open the gates. We always tried to keep up the illusion that the house was inhabited, which at that point it was by two maids, as a lived-in appearance did act as something of a brake to looters. To the Iraqis and, sadly, to many Palestinians empty houses were an invitation to thieve. We suspected that the house searches, which had begun in many districts, were partly to establish which ones were and which were not occupied, so that they could be robbed at night with impunity.

In school there was little we could do to make the place more secure beyond locking and bolting doors. The gunfire and frequent explosions had meant that few guards still remained, for many had joined the refugees. Once more I realized what a safe, reliable place Kuwait had been. The school and for that matter most other buildings in Kuwait, private or otherwise, had been built with relatively little regard for security. Wherever possible fences had been placed round the building to counteract the feeling of a school with high walls that appeared like a prison. With its larger, more cosmopolitan population, Kuwait was a less law-abiding place than it had been 30 years before, but even though their windows were hung with gold gem-encrusted bracelets, necklaces and other valuables, shops in the gold souk rarely needed security guards. Merchants could still leave their shops open and in some markets a cloth was just thrown over the merchandise when the owner was elsewhere. Now suddenly and despairingly I could see how easy it was to climb a wall, walk through a door or push open a gate. For the first time I wished for high solid walls, preferably with barbed wire around them, and even wasted time wistfully imagining such things.

Various schemes flashed through my mind and fleetingly I considered hiding valuable computers, musical instruments, laboratory equipment — the list was endless — down in one of the basement gymnasiums. Perhaps we could then block off the doors and the railed gallery that looked down into the gymnasium. If it could be done it had to conceal a very large area. But even assuming that one could escape the curious eyes of the ceaselessly patrolling army trucks, where were all the bricks with which to do this, or the wooden panels to make it look natural and as if nothing were there? Unable to solve the problem and in answer to a question put to me, I instructed the staff to leave the pictures of the Amir and Crown Prince hanging on the wall in the main administration block and not to disturb the two Kuwaiti flags fluttering from their flag posts out in the yard. We resented feeling that it might really have been more sensible to remove them and that leaving them there would be a provocation to the Iraqis.

Another problem was what to do about our museum, which displayed a large variety of Arab/Islamic artefacts ranging from ceramics to costumes and textiles. We knew that the Iraqis had headed straight into the National Museum along the seafront. This housed the splendid Islamic collection loaned to the nation by Sheikh Nasser and his wife Hussa Al Sabah. In addition, the museum complex housed important Greek and Bronze Age artefacts from Failaka Island, known as Ikaros at the time of Alexander the Great. This small inhabited island with a long history possessed many significant sites dating back over 3000 years. Archaeologists had uncovered much evidence of trading between Sumeria (ancient Mesopotamia), Bahrain and Mohenjodaro, in what is now Pakistan. Placed as it was between Bahrain and Sumeria, Failaka Island must have always been an important stopping-off point for cargo ships, for it had water and had been pleasantly covered in trees. It appears to have been more or less continuously inhabited right up until the invasion by Iraq. Latterly, during excavations by French archaeologists, the site of a Nestorian Church (*c*.400 AD) had come to light in the middle of the island. The Nestorians were a heretic group who broke away from the Byzantine form of Christianity. The sect spread in Persia and to this day its rites are followed by members of the Assyrian faction now living mainly in the north of Iraq.

One section of the National Museum gave visitors an idea of what Kuwait had been like before the oil era and another displayed paintings by Kuwait's modern artists. Near the museum was a merchant's house built some 60 years ago, with some of its decorations showing an art deco influence. It exhibited *sedu* (Bedouin weavings) and

Bedouin women were encouraged to continue their craft there and to sell what they produced. They held weaving classes for adults and children and would come in and work on the looms, allowing interested visitors to watch them.

Kuwaiti artists in the country and a young woman who worked in the Islamic section, Yasmin al Mutawa, had promptly tried to get into the complex to find out what was happening. Most could barely go beyond the entrance, though one person managed to reach the new Iraqi 'director' in his office. He rather loftily remarked that under its new management he hoped the museum would be able to put on an exhibition about Mesopotamia. The Iraqis were rather interested in ancient Mesopotamia, for Saddam was given to comparing himself both with the great Ayoubi period leader, Saladin, who had been involved with Richard the Lion-Heart during the Crusades, and with the biblical figure, Nebuchadnezzar. Bricks on which Saddam's name had been impressed alongside that of Nebuchadnezzar had recently been made to replace old ones on buildings in Babylon. When we had driven through Iraq in mid-1989 we had with some astonishment seen a few of these bricks.

People driving past the National Museum wondering what was going to happen reported that trailers and juggernauts parked outside were being loaded with cartons and then moving off towards the road to Iraq. An order had been issued in Iraq that every province had to contribute some 50 trailers or juggernauts a month in order to 'redistribute' what was removed from 'the nineteenth province'. There were certainly more than that, for all trailers in Kuwait were immediately commandeered by the Iraqis. Besides the tanks and army equipment ploughing along the roads, there were endless lines of trailers heavily loaded with every imaginable object from public buildings, hospitals, clinics, institutes and shops. This mass movement of government and private property into Iraq continued without a halt until a couple of days before the liberation. Indeed during the air war people were reluctant to go into their basements because they knew the soldiers would take the opportunity to break into and loot any empty house.

With all the pillaging going on it was obvious that our museum had to be kept closed. The signs above the doorway were quickly taken down and the heavy carved Indian doors at the entrance were bolted as securely as possible. Then Nadr and I stared up at the entrance and wondered what could be done to make it unobtrusive, but once again it seemed impossible to make it appear just a plain wall. Fortunately the museum was below ground level in two large connected basements under my house and my son's next door. After going down a flight of steps and entering the main section through another beautiful Indian door the visitor is led to the left. There the Koran and manuscripts and ceramics are displayed. The aim of the manuscripts is to illustrate the development of Arabic calligraphy, which is second to none and which was the major Islamic art form. The galleries on the right house textiles and costumes and a large display of intriguing and beautiful silver folk jewellery — once worn so proudly and frequently made with loving skill. How was it that some of the bracelets worn in parts of Saudi Arabia so closely resembled those of Viking and Celtic Britain? The one feature the varied costumes had in common was a tendency to being loose-fitting, otherwise, within the tradition, the combinations of materials, colours and embroideries expressed the imagination and creativity of their owners. Hanging from invisible nylon threads in a long glass gallery were some musical instruments, all with their feeling of warmth and pleasure. Having been working instruments, most had taken on something of the ambience of their original owners in their happiest moments. The atmosphere in the museum reflected that warmth and tranquillity and coming up the stairs out into an increasingly ugly real life was not at all a pleasant experience. It seemed terrible that those beautiful objects, a part of the heritage of the Islamic world, might easily be destroyed, especially as many objects were unique and irreplaceable.

Nadr and I went down the steps into the museum and walked around trying to decide what to do with the exhibits. We had boxes in a store room nearby and plenty of tissue and newspaper. A start could be made and we decided to set to and pack up the side containing the manuscripts and ceramics. Although the school maintenance men and carpenters were leaving they came in to help with the packing. Some of them knew how to pack these items, for they had been taught to do so by my husband. Other staff who had been able to pass by came in and lent a hand as well. The scene was one of frantic though purpose-ful activity, for no one knew when undesirable people might chance past; the guard upstairs was watching the road so that he could warn us if it appeared we might receive unwelcome visitors. What frightened us was the thought that if soldiers did come down they would be likely to tear the museum apart and then set fire to the building when they left.

The museum, which had been open to the public for eleven years, had been designed by my husband and built by the school's Pakistani carpenters and maintenance crew, some of whom were now helping us pack. I wished that my husband were down there with us, instead of being stuck in Amman — we needed his advice on the best, quickest way of packing the fragile ceramics. Amazingly, nothing was broken, even though the objects had to be packed in considerable haste. In the hurry of opening a display case, one worker cut his hand badly on its heavy glass frame and sat down bleeding and in a weak state until he could be taken to hospital for stitches. Fortunately the hospital still functioned, even though patients had been literally thrown out and told to go home. Someone came up asking what should be done with a small nineteenth-century grain of rice inscribed with the writer's name and verses from the Koran. Holding out my hand and saying, 'Don't worry I will put it somewhere safe,' I put it away so carefully that it has still not been found! That part of the conversation is still so clear to me, but what happened afterwards has completely faded. With conditions outside deteriorating daily it was essential that we completed the packing as fast as possible. There was little time for niceties, although everyone took care, especially with the old and fragile manuscript sheets.

Finally, within a few days, the packed boxes, old suitcases and bags were standing in piles on the floor. The heavy glass panels were stacked against the walls and all the showcases were now quite empty. The question was where were the boxes and cases to be hidden? Some could go into a small side exhibition room, which could be blocked off and concealed, but the bulk of the others had to be disposed of elsewhere. It was Mr Nasser, the foreman who had headed the original building team, who remarked that behind one of the big showcases was a large space into which most of the cartons might fit. To our surprise there was indeed a space that even had a few shelves running along its walls. When all the boxes were finally carried in and the display cabinet put back in place again it was hard for the average person to see anything other than empty exhibition cabinets. The panels of Islamic coins, a few of the bulkier items and much of the arms and armour were put into a small side room with a fine seventeenth-century carved Indian door, which was then bolted. The carpenters managed to produce from somewhere sheets of wood which they sealed over the doors. These were painted to match the other walls and hung with a few early nineteenth-century David Robert pictures. These pictures by the famous painter of Middle Eastern subjects would probably not attract the Iraqis particularly, though if they reached the basement they might trash them. That risk had to be taken. Now, barring rockets, fires and other misfortunes, half the museum was at least a little safer than it had been.

One last job remained in that section and that was to make the storage cupboards under the display cases look as if they were merely decorative. The cupboards were filled with manuscripts and other objects not on display and there was nothing the Iraqis liked better than to force open cupboards and tear everything in them apart. By the end of the occupation there was not a single drawer, desk or cupboard in the school left shut, locked or unbroken. The carpenters rapidly prepared strips of wood, painted them a paler shade of the dark grey colour of the cases and in record time fixed them firmly and decoratively across all the cupboard doors. It was hard to guess that behind that simple decoration there were manuscripts and other artefacts.

When one part of the museum had been safely packed and hidden, we turned our attention to the textiles and jewellery. The passage connecting the two sections and a small room to the side was blocked off. The men fitted another panel across the opening and cunningly painted it to match the surrounding wall. More pictures were hung and to prevent unwanted visitors coming too close to the false wall a piece of nineteenth-century Syrian furniture was placed in front. Now the unpacked side of the museum posed an impossible problem. There were five or six thousand pieces of displayed jewellery and many costumes, textiles and embroideries, as well as the stringed musical instruments. Each object needed to be wrapped in tissue paper, which we had run out of completely, and packed carefully and individually in so far non-existent boxes. Nearly every person who had helped with the other side was either trying to leave Kuwait or unable to reach the museum. Only Nadr, myself and Rowa, who lived nearby, could attempt this huge job. In addition, there were storage cupboards and drawers at the top of the house filled with textiles. Should they be carried downstairs and placed — where? For a few days we discussed the situation, along with everything else. Rowa maintained that the storage cupboards should be emptied and their contents brought down to the museum. I agreed, at least until I actually looked at the contents and saw how much time and work would be necessary to complete the job. The threat of army house-to-house searches was coming closer and closer and a great deal of time seemed to be spent watching from windows for the ominous trucks and jeeps to turn up. People would ring to say the army had surrounded such and such a district and were going through each house. The only option seemed to be to try and completely block off that whole section; to pretend that it did not really exist.

The now locked and bolted heavy Indian door faced straight onto the road, but without the name above it was just a door of a type that had once been popular in Kuwait. There were still some around even in modern buildings. The walls on either side of the steps were lined with nineteenth-century orientalist paintings and examples of Arab furniture. At the bottom on either side were two large showcases, one containing swords and daggers, the other small inlaid boxes, ceramics and a big neo-Mamluk-style mosque lamp. The showcases were to be left intact, but the orientalist pictures were to be removed, with two of my favourite ones wrapped up and placed behind some chairs in my dining room. The large portrait of Lady Jane Digby el Mesrab, in her Syrian costume with the pillars of Palmyra behind her, had been painted in 1859 by the well-known orientalist artist Carl Haag. Throughout the nineteenth century western artists had travelled to Egypt and Palestine in search of 'exotic' scenes. They were entranced by the quality of the sunshine and light and it influenced many, including Delacroix. Lady Jane had been a famous Regency beauty, somewhat of the calibre of Lady Hester Stanhope but far more romantic. In her middle age she had fallen in love with and married a sheikh from Palmyra in the Syrian desert and had remained with him in Syria until her death some 30 years later. She had lived with the tribe in their tents during the winter months and had a summer house in Damascus. Her grave can still be seen in the Christian cemetery there. We removed all these interesting orientalist paintings from beside the steps and hid them in corners and cupboards elsewhere.

33

On going down those steps some years before a rather supercilious gentleman had thought that these exhibits were the museum. He paused slightly and murmured, 'What a splendid collection you have.' It seemed a good idea to try and develop his notion. We would remove the orientalist pictures, put a few cheap ones in their place and add as many glittery modern brass dishes down the sides of the steps as we could find. Once again we made use of every last panel of wood to cover the heavy door at the bottom of the steps into the museum. In front of that we half dragged and half lifted into place a very large piece of nineteenth-century Egyptian furniture. It was a passable effort and if anyone came asking about the museum we would show them the 'museum' on the steps. If they persisted, they would be taken over to the now empty side and told that everything was out on exhibition. Perhaps it was all rather weak but it seemed to be the best we could manage in the circumstances. Anything might go wrong: we might be bombed, set on fire, or Iraqis who had previously visited it would know it was not true and report us, but we had to make the effort. If we were bombed I hoped that the concrete would fall in on the place and partially save it.

After that, apart from occasionally unblocking the door and checking to see if the air-conditioning was working, I tried not to think about the museum at all. I had the superstitious idea that thinking or even worrying about it would, in a strange way, attract attention and trouble. I put it firmly to the back of my mind and, in any case, there were many other worse matters to contemplate.

Like everybody else, we wondered how the members of our families who had been out of Kuwait at the time were coping. It was yet another of the torments that nagged at the backs of our minds and needed to be kept under control. My eldest son, Ziad, and his family had been staying with friends in Canada; my daughter, Nur, and her children had been taking a well-earned rest in England. Nur, who is a silversmith, had also been about to embark on a short jewellery course at one of the colleges there. Nadr had returned to Kuwait at the end of July, whereas his wife, who was pregnant, was due to have flown back in the middle of August. We knew that they must be frantic with worry. They joined my husband in Jordan to help at the school because, as one might imagine, there were staff shortages. It had not been a pleasant experience, for the great majority of people had supported Iraq and there were many flag-burning demonstrations in the streets and outside the American and British embassies. As most people were distinctly unsympathetic towards the Kuwaitis, arguments were continually breaking out in the school and elsewhere. They did not care to believe that the situation in Kuwait was so bad after the invasion, even when news via letters smuggled in gave some idea of what was happening. There was a general idea that 'Kuwait deserved it', though why any country, least of all Kuwait, should have deserved such a fate seems illogical. In the end the pressure was so great, the atmosphere so bad and my husband so incensed with the general attitude that he sold his shares and moved to London, where it was at least possible to take part in demonstrations and otherwise help to liberate Kuwait.

Immediately after the invasion most public services came to a complete stop and it swiftly became obvious that something had to be done about rubbish-disposal. For a short time during the first two weeks I saw various vehicles moving slowly past down the road and suddenly realized that the young men in them were Kuwaitis who had taken on the job of trying to clear up as much as possible. But within two or three weeks all the rubbish disposal equipment had either been taken to Iraq or trashed and it became impossible to remove it. So instead everyone placed their bags in open spaces and burned them, generally in the late afternoon. We grew to recognize the different plumes of black or grey smoke that polluted the whole of Kuwait. A fierce, thick black one was most likely a fire or the results of an explosion, the lighter grey ones that drifted up and diffused slowly outwards were probably rubbish fires. Kuwaiti men and women immediately volunteered their services. They helped to staff the hospitals, scrub and clean, remove rubbish, run the cooperatives, lift and carry heavy loads and, while supplies of flour lasted, to make the bread in the bakeries. Until the invasion there sometimes seemed to be a split between the generations. The older Kuwaitis, generally cheerful, kindly yet tough people, had done all the jobs of a normal society, but once oil wealth arrived some less pleasant affectations appeared in the population. With the invasion, however, all the old resilience, courage and character resurfaced and everyone somehow held together to suffer, resist and survive the occupation.

Once the museum had been dealt with, Nadr and I felt we had to try and drive to Sulaibikhat to see what had befallen our house there. We had lived in that district for 20 years and moved away only because of the school and museum. As that suburb was in the path of the invading Iraqis we already knew that the house had been damaged in some of the heavy crossfire. Throughout the occupation the soldiers were spread out and heavily dug in along the beach. Like the oil town of Ahmadi, Sulaibikhat had lost its internal telephone lines early on in the invasion and had been experiencing difficulties securing water and electricity supplies. The people remaining there underwent many privations.

Sulaibikhat is by the sea close to the head of Bay of Kuwait and, because that part of the sea is slowly receding, there are extensive mud flats at low tide. Kuwait is well known for the different species of migrant birds that pass through, especially in spring and autumn. The mud flats used to attract pink flamingos and, for a few weeks in the autumn and spring, 300, 400 or even 500 of them could be seen as a pink haze close to the shore. With their heads down they moved slowly along, feeding on the small creatures below the mud. Over the years, however, they began to move further and further away, being disturbed by the traffic on the newly constructed roads, the new houses and increasing population.

With its low sand dunes and salt bushes (a favourite camel fodder), the area at the head of the bay was in its way quite beautiful. Extending beyond the Mutla' Ridge are the Zor Hills, whose highest point is about 400 feet. The land along the top of them and for the rest of the 150 miles or so to Basra in Iraq is mainly flat and gravelly. Years ago women from southern Iraq used to come and scratch a living collecting gravel for sale, which was needed to build houses in expanding Kuwait. In spring Kuwaitis and naturalists would go there to camp and spend the weekend with just sleeping bags, sandwiches and tea. The stars hung huge and low, blinking gently through the very slight haze. There were well-known sites where the little desert iris grew in purple masses and many would spend the night nearby so that they could see and photograph them at sunrise.

The main road to Sulaibikhat is approximately 15 miles from our house in Jabriya. It passes an open area, which becomes a sheep and antiques market on Fridays. Years before there had been an old door

and window market there that used to be a favourite haunt of westerners keen to buy beautifully carved Kuwaiti doors. Some turned them
into coffee tables and they all took them back to their countries when
they left. The road passes some car showrooms, with their multitude
of cars to suit every pocket, eventually reaches a large army camp
complex and, just beyond, if one continues for long enough, is the
beginning of the road to Basra.

Clutching our IDs and in Nadr's car, we set out on the route to
Sulaibikhat. From the very start of the journey there were burnt-out
cars and smashed jeeps littering the road. Pieces of blackened machinery lay scattered across the barriers. It was noticeable that traffic
regulations had completely broken down. Tanks and armoured
vehicles pounded along on the wrong side of the road. Traffic lights
were ignored and cars went at mad speeds. Most of the population
who drove at that time took to driving in the same manner, as it was
hard, if not dangerous, to try and follow proper rules.

Just over the bridge, looking along the road towards the car
showrooms, we came across an extraordinary sight. It was not so
much that the showrooms had been set on fire and were still smoking,
or that shops with their windows broken were filled with people
wandering in and out through the broken glass carrying away whatever
they fancied, or that the fire engines were only just arriving — it was
their policy always to arrive late if the property belonged to a Kuwaiti.
What was different about this scene were the hundreds, the thousands
of destroyed vehicles. Lorries, vans, trailers and cars were everywhere. The road, pavements, even the barriers, were littered with
smoking, already wheelless machines, their bonnets up, some lying on
their sides looking for all the world like dead upturned cockroaches in
an insecticide advertisement. Nadr cursed and swore and, our faces
frozen in horror, we approached the main army camp, Jiwan, where
the scene was, if possible, even worse.

We had already heard something about the battle that had taken
place on invasion day from a relative, a conscript who had been
ordered there in the early hours of the morning. There had been some
confusion, as well as a shortage of weapons, and the ratio of Kuwaitis
to Iraqis was somewhere in the region of 1:33. By 9.30 a.m. the
Kuwaitis had been asked to 'defend Kuwait to your last drop of
blood', and this they tried to do in spite of being outnumbered and

possessing little heavy weaponry. At around 10.00 a.m. the Iraqis mounted a heavy bombardment by mortars, artillery and rockets. Many targets, including the Military College, were directly hit and their structures collapsed totally. Despite these terrible odds the Kuwaitis held the enemy at bay until the early evening, when the battered remnants were ordered to abandon their positions. More than 200 Kuwaiti soldiers had been killed, some of them mere recruits. There had been many individual deeds of brave resistance by Kuwaiti soldiers during that unequal battle. What we saw as we drove by bore out what we had heard, though it was worse than we had imagined. Outside the camp there must have been at least 5000 private and public vehicles in various stages of burned destruction and abandonment. Part of the Ministry of Electricity building on the other side of the road had been blackened by fire, and rockets seemed to have smashed through some of its windows. As far as we could see the inside of the camp was a blackened jumble of twisted concrete and collapsed buildings. On reaching the big roundabout on the road that eventually led to Iraq, we had yet another shock. Lining the road as far as the eye could see were heavy trailers heading for Iraq loaded with Kuwait's property. Sitting on the now dirty litter strewn roundabout were some Marsh Arab women selling fish from red plastic buckets.

It has been reckoned that the Iraqis stole and destroyed some quarter to half a million vehicles and other forms of transport. Although stiflingly boring in its presentation, while Iraq TV still functioned we all watched it closely. We could spot the cars, buses and vans from Kuwait driving around the streets of Baghdad and other cities. Sometimes they even bore their original numberplates.

I very much wanted to photograph the scene of all those wrecked cars along the road to our house in Sulaibikhat, for it was a quite spectacular sight. But I was afraid to do so, partly because of all the police checks, roadblocks and searches, but also because there were some Palestinians in the vicinity who might have reported me. Although many Palestinians joined and fought with the Kuwaiti Resistance, others had supported the invasion and, unless one knew people personally, it was better to be 'safe than sorry'. For some reason that long stretch of road was the only one ever 'tidied' up and most of the cars gradually disappeared. There were many similar to it but nothing quite so publicly indicative of the situation in Kuwait. It is possible that this area was tidied up because the Iraqis briefly considered allowing the Red Cross to visit Kuwait, but it is far more likely that the cars were taken away so that their tyres and engines could be sold in Iraq, where there was an insatiable demand for such things.

In the middle of August it was announced on Iraqi television that there would be auctions in various towns of cars, buses, office machinery of all types and even milch cows. Thereafter, throughout Iraq there were frequent sales of goods that had obviously been stolen from Kuwait. Everyone knew that such quantities of, for example, new office machinery were not normally available to the ordinary person there. Sweets and chocolates that had not been seen in the shops for years suddenly appeared all over Baghdad. Though I never spotted them on television, one ex-student even reported having seen New English School T-shirts being sold on the pavements of Baghdad.

On 16 August we learned that Saddam Hussein had handed back to Iran, in a mere 24 hours, what Iraq had started an eight-year war to get and for which so many had needlessly died. In other words, he returned the waterway on the Iran side of the Shatt al Arab river. For a brief moment in Kuwait hope revived that the Iraqi Army would withdraw. Surely the Iraqi people, usually so aggressive in attitude, would at last rise in fury at having lost so many fathers and sons in a pointless war. If some died in a rising at least it would be with honour. People driving from Kuwait to Basra to try to use the international telephone lines found a ground swell of grumbling but little more than that. Hope of an Iraqi withdrawal quickly faded.

That same afternoon soldiers drove past the school in jeeps, parked them outside and came swaggering into the office. Looking curiously around they ordered all the bus tyres to be removed and handed over to them. The tyres were saved for the time being by a passing senior officer who saw the jeeps parked outside and ordered the soldiers to leave the premises immediately. Until that point parents had continually rung us to ask if we could open the school at the beginning of September. Even with the confusion that still reigned and the continual explosions and shootings, we thought that it might be possible, assuming the pupils could still reach us, to conduct basic classes quietly and unobtrusively in the basement gymnasium. I actually drew up lists of books and a basic programme that could be used. Teachers and those willing to take classes rang in to offer their services and do what they could to help.

But all these ideas proved impracticable and very soon were abandoned because nearly every school in Kuwait, including the government ones, remained shut as a show of protest. Not only were these the wishes of Kuwait's government-in-exile, announced over the radio and through the Resistance, but people wanted to show their intense opposition to the situation. The Iraqi government, however, ordered all schools to reopen on 1 September after the summer holiday and this included 'the nineteenth province'. In Hawalli, some schools with large Palestinian student bodies unfortunately defied the government-in-exile and did reopen and operate until the start of the air war. One person who lived in that district sent his small daughter to school for three days, mainly (and probably unthinkingly) because he did not wish her to lose any educational time. He was shocked at how the classes were now conducted. He complained that all that the children learned were songs praising Saddam, with the rest of the time spent preparing for his birthday celebrations. That was not education and he withdrew her. A few weeks after that the whole family left Kuwait, unable to cope with such problems any longer.

Most government and private school buildings were taken over shortly after the invasion for use as barracks by the Iraqi Army. Systematically and officially they proceeded to remove equipment in lorries and then to vandalize and wantonly destroy everything they could. Others were commandeered by the *Mukhabarat* as detention and torture centres and everyone soon heard about or knew people who suffered or died in them. After liberation the rooms in some buildings were found to have been used as detention centres: instruments of torture (an electric drill, a variety of saws, broken jagged bottles) were found lying on tables, the walls and floors were bloodstained and bits of human flesh were stuck to beds, walls and doors.

Apart from those providing essential services, such as water, electricity, hospitals and fire-fighting, all institutions refused to open. In fact, with the Iraqis so busy looting and vandalizing them, they had little option but to remain closed. The vigour with which the Iraqis pursued this policy seemed to suggest that they intended little in Kuwait to be allowed to operate as before and did not want 'the Pearl of the Gulf' to function normally, even though in their view it was now considered part of Iraq — 'a branch of the root', as the regime now referred to it.

On 17 August the Iraqis ordered all American and British citizens to report to the Regency Palace and International Hilton hotels. This was a chaotic period for westerners, for no one knew quite what was happening. While up to that point most people had kept their heads 'down', some had gone looking for food and two men had rather idiotically been seen openly taking photographs. The embassies appeared unsure of the situation and conflicting advice was sometimes given to those who rang up trying to find out what to do. Most people, and this no doubt included the embassies, had not realized to what extent the Iraqis intended to ignore or twist international law as it suited them.

The two five-star hotels chosen to receive the westerners were sited along the seashore about 20 kilometres apart. Most Americans were advised not to go there at all, but to remain where they were. Some had already taken refuge in their embassy and at one time there were 300 people sheltering there. Others had decided to remain indoors, in effect to hide. The few British nationals who did on their embassy's advice go to the hotels, found no sign of anyone in uniform. Like the hotel staff they were puzzled and bemused by the whole thing. It has never been discovered why, having issued such an order, not a single official came to meet their 'guests'.

At about the same time the Iraqis told a number of nationals who had taken refuge in the Japanese Embassy to leave Kuwait on a bus to Baghdad where, the authorities in Baghdad assured embassy officials, everyone (men, women and children and even non-diplomats) would be allowed to board planes and fly back to Tokyo. What happened instead was that when the buses arrived in Baghdad all the men, some of whom were in poor health, were made hostages and sent off to various installations. Though the women and children were allowed to leave the country, the men were kept as 'human shields' in often unpleasant conditions until they were released in December.

The Iraqis specialized in creating uncertainty, in delaying tactics and in giving unclear answers to questions. They were at the same time often seemingly disorganized. The propaganda put out and the uncertainty created were probably intentional: they were means of instilling fear and of controlling the population. The logistics of feeding and planning for what became an enormous and unwieldy army, with many of the soldiers poorly trained, were enormous. There were obviously massive amounts of imported ordnance — tanks, lorries, artillery guns and trailers moved endlessly along the roads — yet, as far as we could see, the soldiers of the Republican or People's Army rarely or never exercised. Apart from incessant looting, little was done to keep up their morale, although there were informers in each group to report on behaviour. For the lowly soldier food and water were often almost non-existent and, while this was perhaps due to lack of organization, it often seemed as if, in the government's view, men were expendable. This appeared to be particularly true of soldiers in the People's Army, probably less so in the professional Republican Army. We heard that thousands had perished of heat exhaustion and thirst during the actual invasion. It was said that the bodies of those who had died on the way had been kept in the ice rink in Kuwait to avoid having to send them back to Iraq at that point.

The ones who were organized were the dreaded secret police, the *Mukhababarat*. They were well-paid and numerous and it has been said that one was recruited from nearly every family, thus creating a huge network of informers. In any case, they were to be seen everywhere in Kuwait, on street corners, driving around in suspiciously new cars, near mosques, anywhere where people might be, watching and listening to everything.

One of them was related to a child in the school and I met him personally. He was a small round, well-fed ball of a man, probably in his mid-forties. In many ways he was rather undistinguished until one looked into his pale blue Baghdad eyes with their cold humourless gaze. He had seen everything that was monstrous and it was easy to imagine that he fed on beatings and the screams of the tortured. If that description sounds exaggerated and written for a purpose, it is not; it was exactly what came to mind and caused my hair to stand on end. By then I was aware of his true profession and had considerable trouble trying to keep a non-committal, sufficiently polite expression on my face in his presence.

One afternoon we were packing away and putting out of sight everything in our house, for we knew that sooner or later the soldiers would come, ostensibly searching for arms, but in reality to take what they fancied. The less that could be seen lying about the better. As my

42

Arabic was accented and it was obvious I was not a native-born Kuwaiti, I thought it best to remain indoors as far as possible. If I went outside I wore a headscarf and black *abaya*. I did go out, at times quite often, but it meant that I was confined to the house more than usual. It also meant that these house searches, nasty for anybody, had an extra danger in my case.

As we were trying to stuff things out of sight into cupboards and reflecting on the fact that a determined search would miss nothing, the house was shaken by a series of tremendous explosions that seemed to come from the main road beyond and near the school. The windows shook, shuddered and rattled; one or two small bowls fell off a table and crashed to the floor. My first thought was for the school and for those whom I knew were in it. I screamed out, 'I hope that Abu Yaseen is all right.' The explosions were close by, yet it was impossible to pinpoint anything exactly as shells seemed to be whistling around in all directions. For a minute or two I skittered about aimlessly, while Nadr recklessly ran to a brass grille-work window to try and see what was happening. I yelled, 'Get back from the window,' but as he peered outside what appeared to be a large shell swishéd past, drawing his hair straight out with the power of its after-flight. There was then a deafening crash followed by other smaller explosions. At that we threw ourselves onto the floor near some furniture as all hell seemed to have been let loose and what were presumably rockets hurtled around in all directions. Why most buildings remained unscathed was sheer good luck. One or two heavy concrete buildings not far from us had chunks taken out of them, but as far as I know comparatively little material damage was done.

Because so much army equipment travelled along it, the main road alongside the three schools, which the women had walked along on their demonstration and which was near our house, had already been receiving attention from the Resistance. A long stretch of the road was littered with blown-up jeeps and bits of fractured lorries and every afternoon and evening some incident occurred. This one, however, was quite the most ferocious so far and it seemed likely that an ammunition trailer or lorry had been successfully blasted apart. The noise died away gradually, the swish and whistle of armaments diminished and the afternoon returned to its hot, uneasy peace. We picked ourselves off the floor and tore downstairs and out to see what disaster might have overtaken the school. As we ran out the phone began to ring, for people from all over the area had heard and been shaken by the frenzied explosions. It was easy enough to pinpoint their general direction. Young men and women in cars and on foot were beginning to converge on the area to see what had happened. We ran, even in that late-afternoon heat, as fast as we could over to the school.

Because the affected trailer and what appeared to have been a lorry were Iraqi, army vehicles and fire engines were already arriving, though there was little left to be seen other than scattered and black-ened skeletal remains. Anything human must have been blasted into infinity. Looking sneakily around and aiming quickly, I managed to take a rather poor photograph, which would be of little interest to a casual observer, but did mean something to us. As we ran I could see that most of the windows in all three schools had been shattered. In one of our chemistry laboratories an entire fitment had been forced back into the room, one part landing unbroken on the floor, the other pitched rather elegantly and smashed over the edge of a laboratory table. We were even more amazed to see what had happened to the back door of the basement armchair theatre. It was quite a stout door and had been securely locked. The blasts tore it open, spun it round completely on its hinges and brought it to rest nearly in its original position, only backwards. In addition, an entire window, including its frame, had blown inwards and was lying unbroken on the floor of another part of the building.

As we reached the main entrance, Abu Yaseen (the old man who had worked with us for many years) and a few of the guards staggered out of the basement gym to which they had run for shelter. The school buses and some staff cars had been parked for the summer holidays in the large yard, which was now splattered everywhere with shrapnel and horribly big bits of still hot vicious-looking metal. Unbelievably, most of the shrapnel had actually fallen alongside or between the closely packed buses, though one or two now had punctured tyres and a few had holes in their sides. A live shell, large, silver and shiny, lay glinting in the sunlight in the gutter by the gates. Everyone was shaken but uninjured, though they had been covered in black smoke and more or less had to feel their way into the gymnasium. That experience caused most of the remaining Egyptian guards to join the exodus of refugees, though some remained in Kuwait until the very end. After this particular incident, in which a few houses had been hit and, worse, the Iraqis had threatened to kill everyone in the area if anything like it happened again, the Resistance tried to protect ordinary civilians by keeping its explosions further away from residential districts.

Army vehicles and installations still continued to be attacked, especially along the main roads. Tanks, buses and troop carriers were ambushed and soldiers took to walking in groups and looking nervously behind them. As well as taking up arms, Kuwaiti women distinguished themselves as couriers and weapon carriers. Wofa Al Amir, a young X-ray technician, took part in the bomb attack on the Kuwait International Hilton which housed many important Iraqi officials. She was eventually caught, tortured and strangled to death with a length of wire by the *Mukhabarat*.

With thousands of soldiers in Kuwait, the army outnumbered the local population. The Resistance must have felt like David fighting Goliath, but it at least showed the Iraqis that they were not wanted and that the population refused to be passively subdued. Iraqi soldiers soon became afraid of the people, particularly at night. Despite a general night-time curfew, soldiers' bodies were frequently found, especially in districts like Rumaithiya and Jabriya, where large numbers of Kuwaitis lived. Certainly in Jabriya, shot, garrotted or stabbed bodies of dead soldiers were continually being discovered in the early mornings. Added to the hunger, thirst and low morale of the average *jindi* (soldier) was the knowledge that they could never be quite sure that death was not waiting for them round the next corner. Even with all the roadblocks, house searches and all-night looting expeditions, the army could never be confident they were safe.

The next day those of us who could went in to school to try and clean up the glass that lay all over the yard and now in so many of the classrooms. Already a thick covering of sand and dust was spread over everything. The chemistry preparation room, with its bottles of potentially dangerous chemicals, retorts and instruments, had had its windows and doors, even its extractor fan blown in. Papers mixed with sharp pieces of glass lay scattered everywhere. The door of the refrigerator containing chemicals that needed to be kept cool had blown open and off and slightly tipped over. All we could do was sweep up glass, block some of the broken windows with wood and put chairs against cupboard doors to keep them closed. But, as it turned out, trying to safeguard or clean the school was a complete waste of time.

The next afternoon, but this time further down the road towards the bridge on the Fourth Ring Road, there was another series of loud explosions, with black smoke rising and fire engines and Iraqi lorries converging on the remains. It seemed as if a large Iraqi bus and some smaller vehicles had been blown up. I went as close as I dared but was unable to take any photographs, even with the zoom lens, so returned down the road and went in to drink some tea with my niece Rowa. She had just been in touch with her friend, Lamia Al Bedr, who told her that a number of Bahrainis recovering from serious operations or receiving treatment for cancer or heart conditions had been turned out of their hospital beds by the Iraqis and had nowhere to go. She had converted basements in two of their houses and would try to look after them there. This she did until it was possible to get them out of the country. The Bahraini government eventually managed to have them transported to Baghdad and then flown as hospital cases back to Bahrain.

Extra firemen were brought to Kuwait from Iraq and any Kuwaiti firemen not out of the country on holiday were made to remain at their posts, for this was, especially now, an essential service. Their job was unpleasant and made more so because wherever they went, even if only to visit a friend, they had to be accompanied by an Iraqi. In spite of this some of the firemen managed to take a few photographs of various events. As one might imagine, they were involved in many traumatic scenes. Later on, when the Iraqis were trying to deny to the world that their army had been involved (officially or unofficially) in massive looting throughout Kuwait, they decided to shoot or 'hang offenders' in public as evidence that looting was illegal. The first unfortunate 'thief' to die in this way was an Iraqi lieutenant-colonel who was hanged in public from a contractor's crane. He was supposed to have disobeyed orders from his superiors.

A Kuwaiti fireman friend had been out on duty with his crew and was trying to rest at the station when an Iraqi officer stomped into the building and ordered everyone to turn out to watch people being lined up and shot for 'stealing'. It was uncertain whether these people were civilians or army, or even what nationality they might be. The firemen, at least the Kuwaiti ones, indicated that they did not particularly want to watch an execution, but were ordered out into the open space. As they reluctantly reached the square they saw six blindfolded men being hustled forward with their hands tied behind their backs. Everyone present had to watch those men being shot by a line-up of soldiers. Another friend in a different part of the city had much the same experience. Having been out searching for food, he was walking up the stairs to his flat when some soldiers came up behind him and commanded him to go back down and watch a similar execution, this time on the seafront.

Conditions at the border posts where various nationals were trying to leave Kuwait were described by some tired, hot and dispirited Lebanese friends who rang Nadr to tell him about their experience. A party of 40 cars, taking what personal possessions they could fit in, had got as far as Jahra (near Mutla' Ridge), where the Iraqis had set up a 'border' post. There they waited in the burning sun (at least 45° C) for seven hours amongst thousands of other vehicles and people. When they finally reached the head of the queue they were told that 'no more papers would be processed that day'. People were made to wait, and wait. Sometimes the long lines would move forward a bit, a little hope was given, and then everybody would be told to return to Kuwait. Our friends did eventually manage to leave, but it took another couple of weeks before they were allowed to drive past that border post to Baghdad and to begin the next round of paperwork.

This type of incident occurred at all border posts, whether into Turkey, Saudi Arabia or even Iran. (Later on in the invasion the Iraqis allowed certain nationalities to cross the frontier to their now 'great and good friends' the Iranians.) Once it became clear that the Pakistani government did not intend to support the Iraqis, their refugees were made to wait at borders for days, sometimes weeks. Many gave up, turned round and came back to Kuwait. Needless to say there was little food available, less money and an excellent chance that their cars would be stolen, any money on them removed and that they would be left destitute. There were not just men but women and children in these vehicles and the weather was either blisteringly hot or becoming cold as they moved into the mountainous terrain. The Pakistanis were not allowed to drive the much shorter, less dangerous route to Pakistan across the Basra/Iran border. They were told to obtain their exit permits from Baghdad, drive on northwards to Turkey and then, if they managed to get out of Iraq, they had to go along the cold mountainous route across Turkey, down into Iran and on to the border with Pakistan. This was double the drive from Basra to Pakistan in cars loaded with family and some food for the journey.

Some Pakistani friends of ours who were in a queue at the border post saw a party of Pathans (a martial people known for their hair-trigger sensitivities) trying to leave Kuwait. When the Pathans finally reached the head of the queue and were forced to bow and grovel before the Iraqi soldiers, their papers were dismissed as 'insufficient' and they were turned away. No doubt they had not seemed nearly humble enough. The Pathans returned to Kuwait town with their dignity much injured and were reported hunting for weapons so that they could go and kill all the Iraqis! A large group of Filipino men also arrived after having been forcibly separated from their women and children who had been pushed into Saudi Arabia. The men were not allowed to leave but kept behind to dig foxholes for the Iraqi Army. We never found out what happened to all these people.

News of how the occupation forces were behaving did not immediately reach the outside world, for newspaper and television reporters were not at first allowed into Kuwait. On Iraqi television I sometimes saw interviews by foreign correspondents in Baghdad that seemed to be giving a sympathetic report. I wondered why they had not insisted on being sent to Kuwait. This set us all thinking about how we could send out letters or tapes telling those outside what was really happening. An occupation can never be a pleasant experience, but generally, although there is fighting, resistance and obviously killing, this was something more than that: it was not an occupation at all but a siege. One night, as I was once more hiding away things belonging to friends whose houses were being looted, I chanced on an Amnesty report on torture in Iraq. Flipping open the pages it seemed almost as if its authors had been writing about what was going on in Kuwait. I recognized the beatings with lengths of wire, the broken bottles pushed up orifices and the blood donations compulsorily taken from children. I hid it away again for it was not something to be left lying about.

Months later I received a letter, written in November 1990, which, while acknowledging that the invasion must have been unpleasant, assumed that once that bit was over, the shops opened, business resumed and life returned more or less to normal. It was quite the opposite — life got worse daily and everyone went from crisis to crisis. We began to realize that there was a strong possibility that we might all die in a variety of frightening ways. In spite of that people continued to resist both actively and passively and somehow I, at least, was convinced that the whole situation had to turn in Kuwait's favour.

Various routes and schemes were developed for sending letters and tapes to the outside world. Some Palestinians and other fleeing nationals were willing to hide them in their luggage, down the sides of their cars, or in body belts around their waists. Small tapes were much preferred, for they were easier to keep out of sight. Agreeing to take letters carried a considerable risk, for if caught the penalty was imprisonment or death. Those willing to carry such post were told what was written in it. One person plaintively asked why the letter could not just say we were all well and safe. He received a lecture to which he listened patiently and after that carried scores of written messages to Jordan and returned a number of times with post as well as food. At first the Iraqis did not know what was happening, but they began to realize that news of conditions in Kuwait was reaching the outside world and took to conducting lengthy car and bus searches. A few of these letters were never delivered, but on the whole they eventually reached their destinations and were passed on to organizations like the British Ministry of Defence. In spite of such dangers and though they were infrequent, letters and tapes did go out and occasionally answers arrived along with supplies of food. It was just like Christmas when precious mail arrived with chocolate, flour and baby milk, which would be passed on to people with small children. When the British and American men were in hiding quite a lot of post would arrive. When this happened one would ring a given number, casually and quickly mention that 'there was something to collect' and someone would appear at an arranged time. After carefully glancing around to see that no interested people were watching, the parcel containing the letters would be handed over and taken to the men in question, who would probably be hiding in air-conditioning ducts or a supposedly deserted flat or house.

August was normally a month many people spent outside the country because of the heat. But as far as I was concerned, in these days of air-conditioning, it was a quiet, calm period, with still a month to go before school reopened. The carpenters would be at work, going from classroom to classroom completing repairs or sometimes renovations. New books would arrive from the port in a trailer, along with the kindergarten equipment and paper — coloured tissue. I especially liked the coloured sparkling pieces, which little fingers would make into patterns on sugar paper. It was exciting to look at the different books that arrived, to see how over the years subjects like chemistry had changed and what had once been studied at university level was now part of an ordinary secondary school syllabus. It is important in education to find a balance between what can be made really interesting to learn and what simply has to be committed to memory no matter how boring — like multiplication tables! The basics need to be absorbed so that later on the more interesting parts can be introduced.

The beach clubs would be filled with sunbathers, even though it was the hottest month and, unless there had been sand storms, swimming was not at its best. Being shallow, the waters of the Gulf heated up and bathing felt like stepping from an oven into tepid soup. If there were sand storms, and in some years they could be almost continuous, the sea cooled down miraculously, but then one came out covered in a fine coating of sand, with the backs of one's legs tingling from the grains hitting them. In pre-air-conditioning days August had been a really trying month, with an exhausted population towards the end of it watching for the star, Canopus. It was believed that once that had been sighted (and everyone watched for it) the weather would rapidly begin to cool down. This may or may not have been true, but so hot was it by that time, day and night, that when Canopus did appear one was psychologically prepared to believe that the weather was becoming more temperate. August had of necessity been a quiet month, with the men out on the pearling banks and the women, half stupefied by the intense heat, awaiting their return. No matter what the hardships of the past, August 1990 was quite the most terrible August in the history of Kuwait. The utter confusion and horror of what had happened will linger long in everyone's memory.

4

Into Hiding or be a Hostage

ONE afternoon towards the end of the month Nadr began to set up and conceal his computer equipment in a small room behind the costume cupboards at the top of our house. These cupboards run down the side of an exhibition area and, because they have a panelled decoration, it is not easy to guess that there are rooms behind them. A determined search would have revealed the cupboards and direct hits from bombing would have destroyed them, but once more we were fortunate. Nadr set up a programme through which he managed, with the use of radio waves, to obtain a good deal of official news about what was happening in the Gulf crisis.

As Nadr carried equipment into the small area available to him, I could hear the telephone ringing and ran downstairs to answer it. It was Keaton Woods, the American general manager of the Meridien Hotel. His wife Jinn and their two small children had left the shelter of the American Embassy a few days before and were now living in my son's house next door. Like most women and children they were in effect hiding, for there was uncertainty at that point about women being taken as hostages. A friend of ours, Kirsty Noman, a conservator at the National Museum who had been caught by the Iraqis attempting to escape through the desert by car, had already been sent to what had been the Bechtel camp in Ahmadi. Everyone in this camp, which housed women and children as well as men, was a prisoner and they organized themselves as such.

Jinn's Filipina nanny and maid were both trying to decide whether they should attempt to leave the country. Conditions at their embassy were appalling, for literally thousands had come to try and take refuge there. Innumerable cars, buses and vans, hung with blankets and sheets to try and give shade, were parked in the sun outside. Food was in extremely short supply, money even more so and the only water available was from the taps inside the embassy. Approximately 15,000 people wanted to leave Kuwait. The embassy was just up the road from the Jabriya police station, where shooting still continued at intervals, and the army moved around aggressively in that particular area. For the present, rather than join the masses suffering nearby, it seemed better for the two women to wait and see what happened.

Keaton had been woken early in the morning of 2 August by his secretary phoning to say that Iraqi tanks outside her apartment were shelling the Amir's palace further down the road. He dressed rapidly and went down to the lobby, where he ordered all doors to be secured except for a small side one. At that point the Iraqis had made little effort to come inside and, to discourage soldiers from wandering in, two huge jars of water were placed outside for their use. While the shelling was going on guests were taken down to the basement and, later on, after a soldier had tried to rape one of the female employees, Keaton made sure that all women, guests or otherwise, were kept out of sight elsewhere in the hotel.

The Meridien Hotel is located in the centre of town on the corner of the main road heading towards the Dasman Palace and a road running parallel to the seafront, so a lot of traffic passes near it. Keaton had been in trouble spots before, his last posting being the China of Tiananmen Square. Unlike most of us, he had been paying attention to the news and, alarmed by what he had been hearing, in mid-July he quietly ordered in extra supplies of rice, flour and canned food for the hotel stores. So, for the time being, the hotel was able to offer its guests a reasonable menu and a place of comparative safety.

Some 10 days after the invasion the Iraqi colonel in charge of that district ordered the hotel to accommodate an important government delegation arriving from Baghdad. They would also need to be fed and it still seemed better to keep the original guests out of sight of the new arrivals. By Sunday 19 August Keaton knew that westerners were being picked up at checkpoints, transferred to various hotels and not allowed to leave. If this were happening it was obvious that the Meridien's western guests should somehow be dispersed to safer places. Most of their various embassies agreed to shelter them until the situation became clearer. At the same time many of the hotel's international staff decided that they wished to leave Kuwait and began making arrangements to do so.

On 20 August the Meridien Hotel received orders to house detained westerners. Keaton realized that he too would now have to leave and try to take refuge in the American Embassy, which was already host to between 200 and 300 people. Shortly after his arrival and knowing that food and water would have to be conserved if, as now seemed likely, the electricity was cut off, Ambassador Howell told everyone that, except for eight senior staff, all diplomats would travel in convoy to Baghdad. Non-diplomats could join the group, but it seemed likely that they would be arrested and taken as hostages.

Just before Keaton left the embassy to go on the run once more, he rang up and I was startled to hear a voice asking in fluent French if I could perhaps house a number of escaping people? I was somewhat taken aback because, although I could understand well enough, my French had become rusty from many years of disuse and it nearly deserted me when it came to replying. In fact I was tempted to answer in Arabic, which would not have been a good idea, for embassy lines were almost sure to be tapped. However, the answer was simple enough: of course we were prepared to hide anyone on the run and, with that, Keaton rang off at once.

As in our own house, everything in my son's house had, as far as possible, been packed away in case of house searches. It was also important to give the impression that the place was occupied, which it now was by Jinn, her children and the two maids. It was dangerous to leave women and children alone in a house with the army continually circling around in their jeeps, their eyes interestedly taking everything in. The women kept out of sight as much as possible and were in constant telephone contact in case anything strange happened. Just as I was about to go over to tell Jinn that her husband was coming the phone rang again. This time the call was to pass on the latest rumour, which was that Saddam had been shot dead by the 'red-haired one' (his second wife), as well as the slightly more plausible story that the people in Basra were close to rioting and the life-sized statues of Saddam dotted everywhere had been daubed with black paint.

Those particular French visitors never did arrive, for they were dropped off at other places. Instead, in the middle of the hot afternoon,

Keaton himself appeared. He dismissed his driver at the end of the road as a precaution, walked quickly to the house and slipped through the gates. At that time of day it was quieter because of the heat and even army jeeps were less inclined to be touring the streets.

Keaton and I exchanged our news and he mentioned that the embassy staff was now down to about eight, including the ambassador, the chancellor, Barbara Bodine, and the new consul, Gail Rogers, who had had the misfortune to arrive just in time for the invasion. Like the British ambassador (Michael Weston) and consul (Larry Banks), these people would sit for hours at the end of a telephone line giving advice, passing on messages, trying to work out travel details for women and children when they were allowed to leave and, with the help of wardens and members of the Resistance, arranging to hide as many potential hostages as they could. There must have been literally thousands in hiding at the beginning of the invasion, and by the time the men were released in December there were still around 2000 men in flats, basements, air-conditioning ducts and even under water tanks on the tops of roofs — anywhere in fact where they could remain out of sight. They were supplied with food by the Kuwaitis and other nationals, as well as by Palestinians who were loyal to Kuwait. Regrettably, others were turned in and the contents of their flats removed or sold by those who supported the invasion.

Keaton had arrived with a suitcase and some food he thought might be useful. Over a cup of tea the situation was assessed and discussed, including whether the swimming pool at the top of the house should remain full or be emptied. Keaton thought it should be left full in case of a chemical attack, which, from the start of the invasion, had seemed a possibility. He was thinking of the village of Halabja in Iraq where 4000 men, women and children had died from such an attack. Everyone in Kuwait was filled with apprehension and became even more worried towards the end of August when Saddam Hussein appointed his cousin, Ali Hassan Al Majeed, as the governor of Kuwait. The latter had reputedly been responsible for organizing the deaths of Kurdish villagers by means of toxic chemicals. As was generally known by the world, including the Arab countries, entire communities of men, women and children had been struck down where they stood as invisible waves of poison gases were released over them. Certainly after the arrival in Kuwait of Ali Hassan Al Majeed, the reign of terror intensified, as did the rumours of possible chemical attacks.

After some consideration I decided to empty the swimming pool because the thought of the pool leaking and maybe bursting and flooding all over the house seemed too strong a possibility. Instead we filled all the baths with water and later on sealed the air-conditioning vents in the empty part of the basement, which is what the Israelis did to protect themselves from Scud missiles that were possibly carrying chemical warheads.

Keaton was a splendid person to hide. He was very conscious that being caught could mean death for those who hid him. But we both thought that it was his duty to hide and not to allow himself to be caught, for what the Iraqis were doing was outrageous and illegal and the more people who defied them the better. He set up various cameras to watch the roads, but they had to be hidden away when the possibility of a house search became more likely. He never allowed himself be seen outlined against a window and, knowing that a search could be conducted at any time, was ever on the alert. Few people can concentrate for long under such conditions and this meant that it was impossible to do anything that required one's complete attention. One friend, whose letter got through, commented that at least I could pass the time working on costume research or cataloguing. As I spent most of the day pacing the house watching from the windows (somehow the prospect of a search seemed 'safer' if we were prepared for it) such work seemed unthinkable.

At night Nadr took over. He would run between his 'secret' room full of computers and all the windows to watch for whatever might happen. Everyone listened to the news, watched TV, embroidered, read a little and wrote letters, but always with an eye on what was going on outside and ready to spring into action, hiding radios and all the other things that had now become 'illegal'.

The news from school was alarming. A jeep load of soldiers had already been in and tried to remove the tyres from the school buses. And now a far more official-looking lot, in a police car and wanette filled with heavily armed soldiers, stopped outside, marched in and threatened everyone by saying that westerners were being hidden there. One or two Egyptian guards were there, as well as Abu Ali, Abu Yaseen and a member of the secondary school staff. Abu Ali and Abu

Yaseen had worked with us for years. Both originated from Basra, but had lived in Kuwait for a very long time and had Kuwaiti family connections. They were in a very difficult position because they could be recognized by their accents but had absolutely no sympathy for the invaders. Indeed they were open to insults from the army, who often shouted '*helb Jaber*' (Jaber's dogs) at such people.

As the police stormed into the administration office they immediately saw the pictures of the Amir and Crown Prince. They came to a sharp stop, snarlingly went over to them and ripped them off the wall, trampling and stamping them underfoot until they were in small pieces. They then asked why these portraits had been left hanging on the wall. Abu Yaseen made some sharp reply, for which he was rewarded with a hard cuff across the face and hit with a rifle. Kicking open doors, or shoving them in with the butts of their rifles, they pushed their way into the administration secretary's office. Like most such places these days, the school was equipped with fax machines, computers and a main telephone switchboard with connections all over the school. On seeing all this machinery, the officer angrily bellowed, 'This is a spy room. The people in here are spies.' Most of the soldiers, apart from those at the highest level, were surprised by the range and extent of the electronic equipment in Kuwait and, as I mentioned earlier, they had at first thought that computers were televisions that did not work properly. Mohammed Sofdar, the secondary school clerk, quietly explained to the officer that all schools in Kuwait possessed such equipment and that it was normal in Kuwait.

Abu Yaseen was ordered to take the commanding officer down to the basement stockroom. Having failed to grow with the size of the school, every shelf was well-stocked with equipment and the officer repeated his accusation that this was no school but some kind of a spy communications centre. To this Abu Yaseen once again replied that all schools had stockrooms and that in any case the school had been in these premises for many years, in fact long before 'the Iraq–Iran war'. The commander stopped short, fixed the old man with a furious gaze and replied, 'What Iraq–Iran war? We are great friends, we are family and do not say such things.'

For once Abu Yaseen was speechless and he slowly led the officer out into the yard towards the secondary school office. As the two Kuwaiti flags in the yard were spotted fluttering idly in the hot breeze there was an outburst of more swearing and cursing (unlike most other Arabs, Iraqis are well-known for their casual use of foul language) and the officer ordered the flags to be torn down. On catching sight of one of the Egyptian guards clucking disapprovingly at this display of bad temper, he caught him across the shoulders with his rifle. When the flags had been torn away from their flag poles, the guard, Faiz, was ordered to spit on them, stamp them underfoot and finally to burn them. Faiz, a quiet thin man, was particularly unfortunate because later on, when the Iraqis occupied the school, he was made to go round and remove the Kuwaiti graffiti from all the walls around the school. Although he remained in Kuwait until almost the end, after this he took care to keep well away from the school, for he had absolutely no intention of being made to serve tea to the Iraqis. The Iraqis replaced the Kuwaiti graffiti with plentiful amounts of their own, which were extremely difficult to erase later on. A particularly surprising one read, 'Saddam Hussein, the Champion of Peace and Harmony'.

Towards the end of August we were entertained by the amazing spectacle on Iraqi TV of a British couple, who had apparently been working in a hotel in Kuwait, being married courtesy of Saddam Hussein. I missed the beginning of the wedding and have never since read the UK newspaper reports of it, but turned the programme on as the bride and groom were walking down the aisle of the old church to the reception. It all added to the *Alice through the Looking Glass* feeling of taking part in some mad, unrealistic dream. In fact I had to check that it was a TV programme relayed from Baghdad and not some kind of poor play. It was unbelievable that two supposedly adult people could agree to such a charade. At first I thought they had probably been forced into it, but the bride did look genuinely delighted and at one point she smilingly said that 'had they got married at home, they would probably have been in jeans and T-shirts' and that they would 'always view Baghdad as their second home'.

At the time of the wedding Saddam was shown patting the head of Stuart Lockwood, an obviously petrified young boy amongst the women and children being held in Baghdad. Everyone particularly disliked the interpreter and the smarmy pitch of his voice, especially when he asked Stuart if he had had his milk and cornflakes and then made a quick aside about the children of Iraq having no milk. We knew there had been little milk there for a long time and that most of Kuwait's tinned and fresh milk had been removed to Iraq for the use of the few who could afford it. At the same time as that broadcast was taking place it was officially announced in Kuwait that any Kuwaiti, or for that matter anybody, caught harbouring westerners would be hanged or shot.

In the journal I wrote each day, besides discussing the wedding I noted that my husband's uncle, Sayid Ahmad, had been in hospital with a broken thigh and recent gall bladder operation. Along with many other people, no matter what their state of health, he had been turned out of his hospital bed to make way for 'wounded Iraqi soldiers'. Shortly before Iraqi doctors were sent to Kuwait to take over the running of the hospitals and to change their names to variations of 'Saddam Hospital', Kuwaiti women had begun to help with cleaning, carrying and general hospital work, for most of the original staff had left or were leaving. I was wondering whether I too should volunteer my services when, once again via the telephone, we heard the now famous story about 'babies being thrown out of their incubators'. This occurred some time before the report to the US Congress about human rights crimes taking place in Kuwait. We heard that premature babies had been tipped onto the floor and their incubators taken off to Iraq, but we had no idea of the numbers involved. This incident and others were enough to deter many people from going in to help. People objected, not only to the brusque and generally unpleasant manners of the Iraqi directors and staff being sent to the hospitals, but to the fact that they were threatened with their lives if they did not do exactly as they were ordered — which was in effect to ignore any non-Iraqi patients. One Indian nurse, who commented that she had a duty to treat all people no matter what their nationality, felt unable to put up with what she saw as the uncaring attitude of the new directors and, shortly afterwards, she left the country.

With a window facing the road and overlooking an area of sand where boys used to play football, the kitchen had become the place to sit. From there we could watch what was going on, pick up the telephone, and write letters or work on tapes we hoped to smuggle out. The telephone was by now 'illegal', especially since it was also a fax machine, but we could push it under the shelf where it was less easily seen. I was sitting at the table glancing out of the window one day when there was another series of big explosions and the usual ratatat of gunfire. By now, towards the end of the month, we had become used to gunfire and explosions and it took something more than that to attract our attention. A friend who lived nearer to where the explosions seemed to be coming from rang to say that there had been some kind of 'blow-up' by the bridge on the Fourth Ring Road. Grabbing the binoculars — also 'illegal' — we dropped everything and rushed up to see what we could from the top of the roof. A thick column of black smoke curled into the sky and the sound of sirens shrilled through the air. Smaller explosions spattered around and, judging from the sounds, yet another ammunition truck might well have been blasted into infinity. The Resistance had once again been active and the top of that bridge was eventually closed off to all but army traffic.

Once more the phone rang loudly and this time it was one of our teachers, Kate Craig. She and her husband Bill were on the run from the Iraqis yet again. They had left their flat to take refuge in another one, which belonged to friends out of the country on leave. This flat, which was not far from our house, was 'in the eye of the storm', for it was practically opposite the Jabriya police station.

Perhaps a more accurate way of putting it would have been 'near the eye of the storm', for they had to keep a constant eye, not only on the Iraqi police in the police station, but also on the soldiers patrolling up and down the roads. The soldiers had recently begun a series of house searches in that area and, just before she rang, Kate and Bill had nearly been caught in one of these searches. The soldiers had thumped on their front door, but luckily some Filipinos had held them up for long enough to allow them to climb hastily into the small air-conditioning ducts before the soldiers began to thunder round the house. They were looking for westerners and anything else they could find of value. After a number of hours, half frozen in the ducts on a burning hot day, Kate and Bill managed to get down and escape to the back of the house. They were outside but did not know where to go next. Creeping back into the house to the telephone, Kate asked me in a whisper if I could think of anywhere for them to hide.

I already had Keaton, with his wife, children and two Filipinas, in my house, as well as another couple with two children who were leaving the next day. I couldn't keep Kate hanging on the phone, for they were more or less surrounded by the army. The school was out because far too much attention was now being paid to it. The director's house — not safe, for the Iraqis were now on the roof of the government school very close by and were watching everything that went on. The house in Sulaibikhat was not only far away but had already come under rocket attack. A rather decrepit house about three miles away in Rumaithiya was out of the question because so many people were living in it at that point.

Desperately I cast around for a suitable place. The school flats, which were not too far away, seemed a possibility — they were empty because most of the staff were out of Kuwait at the time. Quickly I asked if she could ring off for a moment and contact me again within five minutes. Our general maintenance man, Mr Khan, lived in those flats with his wife and had been unable to leave Kuwait because she was heavily pregnant. Dialling as fast as I could and with a stroke of luck, I managed to reach him immediately. Being fearful that the phone line might be tapped, I asked if he could get over and speak to me. And, almost before I had put the phone down, he arrived. I told him what had happened and suggested we allow Kate and Bill to shelter in a staff flat. I pointed out that if he and his family were caught hiding westerners they would be in real trouble and that if he felt it was not possible I would somehow think of something else. Without hesitation, Mr Khan replied that he knew which flat would be suitable for people on the run and asked where they were so that he could take them there immediately. The phone rang and Kate was back on the line.

'Can you get over to my house now?' I asked.

'Yes, we're coming; they're closing in again,' and the line went dead.

Mr Khan and I went down to the yard to watch out for any vehicle in which they might arrive. It took longer than expected for the blue Pajero in which they were travelling to arrive, as they had to avoid the numerous roadblocks that appeared out of nowhere. In the end the driver had to climb up and over pavements and sneak through side streets, all the time watching out for sudden road checks. The four-wheel-drive came lurching over the sand and onto the road in front of us. Two terrified and brave Sri Lankans, their faces literally grey with strain, drew to a stop. In the back was Kate, her blonde hair covered with a black scarf and, half rising from the floor and, as Kate later put it, 'being trampled underfoot by me', was Bill, who had nothing with which to cover his blond hair. It had been a nerve-wracking journey, especially since the army was looking for westerners and some Britons had just been caught near them and taken off as hostages, or as the *Raees* (Saddam, the President) now called them, 'guests'. *Dhuif*, the Arabic word for guests, who were so honoured in the Arab world, now had different and less pleasant connotations.

Rapidly I told Kate and Bill where they were going, at least for the time being, and Mr Khan squashed in beside the driver and the other man to show them the way to the flats. They drove cautiously along side roads and when they arrived at the flats they went into the one Mr Khan thought would be the safest. No one appeared to notice their arrival. Everything seemed quiet, the traffic almost non-existent. Mr Khan told them to keep the curtains drawn at all times and never to answer the telephone. This was a wise precaution because the intelligence services and others seemed to be using the phone to find out if places were occupied, to check up on people and to listen in on their conversations. Khan would keep them supplied with food and they could use the television and radio there to keep up with the news. It was a frightening and boring existence because one had to remain on the alert all the time in case the army descended. There was always the possibility that neighbours had seen them coming and would report them. After all, the reward for turning in potential hostages was now 10,000 Iraqi dinars.

Not long after Kate and Bill had left with Mr Khan, Mr Nasser, our Pakistani foreman, came in. He had packed up and taken his wife, children, mother and brothers in two cars on the long road to Baghdad to get permission from the Iraqis to leave the country. On this occasion permission had not been granted, so they had returned to Kuwait. He reported that tanks were rumbling around everywhere, the roads alive with military equipment going south to Kuwait. On the other side of the road the traffic was nose to tail with loaded trailers going to Baghdad. He said that the people in the streets were grumbling about shortages and that the few to whom he had spoken had not thought the invasion a good idea. This story was repeated countless times and, in my naiveté, I at least partially believed the 'Arab brother' myth. I hoped and thought that if the masses did not really approve of the invasion then there might be a general uprising.

61

Or, Saddam would come to his senses and withdraw from Kuwait. Instead I could see people outside making sandbags to put round their windows as protection against the bombing we expected if Iraq did not move out of Kuwait. Little did we realize that the bombing would begin in January 1991, not, as everyone imagined, by the end of September 1990 at the latest. At any rate I too placed food and water and some blankets down in the empty side of the museum and, in case it all happened too fast to get over there, I also put some at the bottom of the stairs.

By the end of August house searches had been conducted in many areas, including parts of Jabriya. Friends rang to ask if we were still safe, but, although we heard about searches every day, so far nothing much had happened in our immediate area. The jeeps continued to roll past, soldiers wandered by and the door to the guards' room next to the locked and bolted museum had been rattled at night, much to the alarm of those sleeping there. I walked over to the rubbish skips at night to burn the piles of refuse. Most of the disposal lorries were now being stolen and taken off to Iraq.

We knew that sooner or later we would probably be subjected to a search and all we could do was watch and wait for it to happen. Occasionally I went out for careful walks, keeping away from anyone in uniform and diving down side streets and into hedges if a sudden outburst of shooting began. Once I went past our director's house, intending to see how it looked. Up until then it was still being cared for by some of the men who worked at the school. Just as I walked round the corner there was a sudden loud rattle of gunfire. It sounded so close that I had to throw myself into a hedge until it gradually came to a stop. I quickly returned home to the accompaniment of gunfire coming from various other but more distant quarters. Arriving back at the house I discovered that the army (once again and the same lot as before) had turned up at school and insisted on being served tea by Abu Yaseen. He and a couple of other men had been trying to guard the school but it was becoming more and more dangerous — and he had no intention of making tea for the Iraqi Army.

As the major sat down he shouted at the old man, 'Why aren't you preparing to open the school — all schools in Iraq [meaning Kuwait as well] will open on 1 September — and where is the owner of the school, Tareq Sayid?' Waving his hands around and no doubt shouting back, Abu Yaseen replied, 'Because of you lot, of course. Look what you've done, ruined everything. How do you think anything can open now?'

This was badly received and earned him another clip over the head. Although it was dangerous to shout or argue too vehemently with the army, on the whole it was nevertheless better to appear confident, for any sign of weakness was immediately seized on and exploited. This did not apply to the *Mukhabarat* — they were dangerous people with a lot of power, who delighted in finding an excuse to beat, violate and humiliate. This is not to say that the army did not behave brutally; it was probably under orders to do so anyway and it often did. But if one were caught by the army one could possibly take certain risks one would never dare take with the *Mukhabarat*.

Things did not seem to be going too well at school and on the grapevine news was coming through that it might well be commandeered by the Iraqi Army for its regiments. While thinking about this horrible prospect and wondering what could be done, I noticed a considerable amount of activity in the direction of the Iranian school at the bottom of the road. It had been a large institution, with one side for boys and one for girls. Like most schools it had not reopened, yet there were cars, vans, lorries and many people, men and women, milling about and appearing worried and anxious. Shortly afterwards some Iranian friends arrived to stay and we discovered the reason for all this activity. Most of the Iranian nationals had decided to return to their country, which they were now able to do over the border from Basra. They did not have to go to Baghdad for an exit visa because, as the commander in school had informed Abu Yaseen in the stockroom, 'they are our friends'. However, the Islamic Republic of Iran was not taken in; its nationals did not wish to stay under the present circumstances and the Republic was continuing to insist that Iraq should withdraw from Kuwait.

The Iranian community numbered about 50,000 people, who ranged from high-powered businessmen to the bakers who made the delicious *khubiz Irani*, or Iranian bread. Every morning and evening patient queues of people would wait to buy the hot flat unleavened bread as it came out of the special ovens dotted all over Kuwait. They would then rush home with their warm pile and eat it, still hot, with fried eggs, or a concoction of cooked tomato and eggs, or just on its own. It was one of the pleasures of life and had been made in Kuwait for as long as anyone could remember.

For the next week or so the whole road was crowded with people (their cars, vans, or lorries loaded with their possessions) waiting to move off at night in convoy. This they did starting at about 2.00 a.m., with the last van at the tail end having usually left by around 6.00 a.m. No doubt they travelled at night to avoid the heat of the day as far as possible and, since there was a curfew, they must have had permission to travel at that time.

Allied and Iraqi news coverage on radio and television was compulsive viewing and most people in Kuwait were able to watch the news until the electricity finally failed. In theory a satellite dish (which we did not have) was illegal and some were removed or broken by the Iraqis. A Lebanese family living opposite a police station had been watching the news on their screen when there was an outburst of shooting aimed directly at their house. They threw themselves flat on the floor to avoid being hit should the glass shatter. Shortly afterwards the Iraqis from the police station were banging on their door, demanding to know why they had allowed Kuwaitis onto their roof to shoot at them. Puzzled, the man of the house replied that only his family were in the villa. Suddenly he realized what must have happened. Switching channels on the television made the satellite click noisily as it changed direction and this could have sounded like shooting to nervous policemen whose station was often attacked in the evening. When he demonstrated this to the police they were able to see that, at least on this occasion, no one had been aiming at them. They were so keen to get outside news themselves that they made the owner hand the satellite over to them for their own use. Perhaps they got another perspective on what was happening in the wider world.

Although we did not have a dish we could tune in to Bahrain, Dubai, Qatar and Saudi Arabia, all of which had good coverage and seemed to be coming through very clearly. On one occasion our spirits were lifted by catching sight of my older son at a big Kuwaiti demonstration in the UAE. Although the news was interesting, indeed fascinating, it could also be very depressing. We watched endless analysts who we sometimes thought assessed the situation wrongly. We watched the rather undignified sight of statesmen and former prime ministers going to Iraq to try and get some of the hostages released, with the Iraqi regime making every possible propaganda use of the coverage. There were peace activists, including ex-pop singer turned Muslim, Cat Stevens, and the CND's Pat Arrowsmith, who were living in the desert in Iraq with other activists so that they could stand between the Coalition and Iraq if war broke out. While killing and war were the last things anyone in Kuwait wanted, we wondered if words of peace were much use to the Iraqis, who had such different intentions. We also wondered how these activists might have felt had they been in our position, expecting every day to die from possible starvation, torture or plain outright murder. Did they really feel that the probable death of over 250,000 people was just a small matter? We did not particularly want to be a sacrifice to the idea of peace. That whole period, including the air and ground war, was unique in world history. For the first time it was possible to watch the bombing of Baghdad as it happened. One of our teachers who had been in Bahrain at the time later told me that she had simultaneously watched a Scud missile approaching Dhahran on her television set and looked out of her window to catch a glimpse of the actual Scud heading for its target.

We were aware that sanctions were not working properly because a small box of Jordanian tomatoes, round and red, cost 27 Kuwaiti dinars (KD), while a similar box of Iraqi ones, misshapen and with black spots on them, fetched KD 9. We also suspected that things other than food were arriving in Kuwait in the trailers. One of the Jordanian drivers we knew hinted as much, but we had no means of proving it. None of us really knew what was going to happen next, but we did all know that August had been the most horrendous month it was possible to live through.

On the last day of that month I wrote in my journal:

House-to-house searches were taking place all over Kuwait and seemed to be coming nearer and nearer to our area. If only the Iraqis would withdraw, was my constant but increasingly unlikely hope. I must admit to being somewhat jumpy and given to staring compulsively out of the window and searching for Red Berets [Republican Army soldiers, the professional men]. Any sight of one causes indrawn breath and a second when the heart seems to stop. I rush to the window and stare out as anything on wheels goes by and slows down near the corner. My friend Gladys [a colleague at school] rang up to say that 31 Brits had been picked up by the army at the Turkish restaurant in Salmiya where they had been hiding. She also mentioned that a large number of British (?) military men presumably from KLT [Kuwait Liaison Team] had been hiding along with some women and children in a basement in one of the sports stadiums. Someone informed on them, for the place was suddenly surrounded by the Iraqis and they were taken away to the Regency Palace Hotel to await transportation to Baghdad. One of the wives had phoned Gladys from the hotel to tell her what had happened.

PART II

Siege
September 1990 to 16 January 1991

5

Rooftop Protests at Midnight

THE nightmarish month of August had come to an end. Each new day brought not withdrawal of troops and freedom but more apprehension. For those in hiding every day must have seemed like a refined form of torture. Kuwait was virtually in a state of siege, and one way or another most of the population were really prisoners or, if westerners, in hiding. Not only British, American or French nationals were forced to go underground. There were others also, such as an Egyptian bank manager who refused to impart information about his bank to Iraqi officials who came in demanding all kinds of details about its operations. He had to move hastily out of his house, find another place and remain in hiding. For some, the Kuwaiti Resistance managed to forge very effective false identity cards. Many Kuwaitis went into hiding as well, moving from place to place just one step ahead of being captured. If they were in the army, the CID or the police, if they had connections with anyone in these jobs, or if they belonged to the large Al Sabah family, they were in great danger. One of our young relatives, a recent graduate of the police college, had had to go on the run. He eventually managed to escape over the border just as he was on the point of being caught. Those who were caught could at the very least expect to be imprisoned and severely beaten up.

Theft and looting continued right up until the last moments of the occupation — even embassy premises were often ransacked. Three of the four recently completed buildings yet to be rented out in the fairly new embassy compound were looted and burned; the fourth was where Saddam's son, Oddai, stayed on his visits to Kuwait. It was filled with

69

splendid furniture taken from other houses: its basements were also filled, presumably with furnishings waiting to be transported to Iraq.

A soldier coming out from a house search clutching a radio cassette he had picked up was asked if he was going to take it back to Iraq. 'No,' he replied. 'No, I'll play the cassettes until the batteries run out and then throw it away.' This seemed to be a typical attitude. Who got what in the army appeared to be graded by rank, with mere soldiers mostly allowed to take the cheaper objects and so on up to the higher echelons. When the army was shifting heavy dental machinery from the main government dental clinic, the labourers rolled it carelessly downstairs, watched by the professional managers sent in from Iraq to oversee the removals. Much of the equipment removed from such institutes seemed to be broken or unusable before it ever reached its destination in Iraq, which makes what was done even worse. Had it at least been useful to other people it would have been better than this mere wholesale destruction.

On one occasion I watched soldiers enter a house in which the sole occupant at the time was an Indian gardener. He protested, but was pushed roughly aside as they went through the gate. Shortly afterwards a group of the soldiers tottered out with an air-conditioning unit and shoved it into an army pick-up. A young *jindi* strolled out clutching a child's brightly coloured plastic melodion. He walked across the sand playing it, suddenly got tired of the whole thing, tossed it onto the sand and wandered back into the house to hunt for something better.

Mr Khan had gone out to the house in Sulaibikhat to see if he could do anything to make it more secure. As it lay just off the direct road to Mutla'a Ridge and Basra, he was able to see the massive traffic going towards Iraq. The outgoing traffic was, as it had been for the past month, nose to tail with loaded lorries and trailers, pick-ups and cars, new and old. The incoming traffic consisted of empty trailers and an assortment of military vehicles. Iraqi men and women were still going back and forth to engage in one form or another of doubtful business. One Iraqi woman from a well-known family in Baghdad came on a visit because she wanted to 'do some shopping' and was most annoyed to find that this was impossible. It was politely suggested she return to Baghdad as she might *now* find what she required there. The Marsh Arab women who had come down from Basra with plastic buckets of river fish for sale were still sitting on the large central roundabout that leads to the direct route to Iraq.

Since the Gulf crisis most people have heard of the marshes in southern Iraq, which cover an area of about 10,000 square miles. It is, or was, a place of watery beauty, a world made up of tall rustling reeds with paths cut through by the streamlined marsh boats. In it live the so-called Marsh Arabs on their man-made floating islands of reeds. They construct their dwellings out of the reeds, each place with a guesthouse or *mudhif* for visitors. A *mudhif* can be of cathedral-like proportions. The shapes and patterns of these intricately woven reeds are reminiscent of those of Sumerian times (3500–2500 BC). In addition to fishing, these people also breed water buffalo, which give a rich milk and an even richer cream. The women used to walk to Basra every day with trays filled with small dishes of cream, which they would sell to their particular customers. The marshes were famous for their bird life and, strangely, for a much-feared and vicious wild boar. It could grow to six feet in length and would crash out of the reeds at tremendous speed, slashing at everything in sight with its long razor-sharp tusks. Any person in its path would be unlikely to survive the slashes and trampling. In happier days the marshes were a popular hunting ground for Americans and other westerners, who would go into them with a guide in pursuit of duck and boar. The marshes seem to have been populated since far back in history and many rebellions have been conducted from them. A slave rebellion (*Thawrat-il-Zenj*) in the ninth century had at first been quite successful but was eventually crushed by the government of the day. People on the run have always gone into the marshes to hide. As a result, and frequently deservedly, the inhabitants had not had a very good reputation. It was some of the women from the villages on the fringes of these marshes who had taken the opportunity to come in to sell their fish.

As practically all the shops and stores remained closed, unattractive and dirty street markets had suddenly sprouted all over Kuwait, as well as on the roundabout. Alongside the Marsh Arab women selling their fish were all kinds of people who, having run out of money, were selling electronics, old clothes, cigarettes, or anything else that was saleable. The spirals of smoke — black ones from the trailers, jeeps or lorries blown up by the Resistance and mere wispy ones from the sprawling burning rubbish tips — were still curling up all over

Kuwait. On nearing a rubbish tip, a swell and heave in one corner would be followed by the eruption and speeding out of sight of soot-covered, sharp-eyed cats. One hesitated to burn the tips completely, if only to give the cats a chance to find something to eat.

A friend's cat, a big placid orange feline, had to fend for himself for the first time in his life and managed to survive the ordeal. At first the houseboy had fed him, but he eventually joined the flow of refugees. After that friends took the cat to their house. Then one day the army threw a man's dead body into their garden and they too had to leave. Unable to find the cat, he was left behind. He spent the next months alone, 'his' house looted a number of times, foraging as best he could. He is now back with his original 'family' and is still as loving, perhaps more so, and as placid as he ever was. One thing is different, however: food can no longer be left out where he can get at it, because no matter how well or recently he has been fed, he cannot resist stealing. If he can, he will creep up to the food, a paw will sneak out quickly and the morsel is dragged away. In a sense, like everyone else he has been traumatized.

Cats are great survivors and it was probably the dogs that suffered most. For the first few weeks of the invasion one could see all types of 'house' dogs running jauntily around the tips, scuffling here and there with their tails waving about in delight at their 'freedom'. Gradually they began to disappear until only those with a real survival instinct remained, now thinner and much scruffier. Normally when their owners are on holiday there is always someone (a neighbour, a friend or a servant) to see that they have food and water. One beautiful golden retriever suffered a terrible death. The family had gone on holiday and, as normal, the maid had stayed behind to look after the dog. The Iraqi Army was thickly congregated in that particular area and the maid eventually fled in panic because it was dangerous for a woman to stay there on her own. In her fear and haste she left the dog in the bathroom with plenty of food and water, mistakenly assuming that the crisis would not last for long. She should really have turned the dog onto the streets where it might have survived. At any rate it died on the bathroom floor, in the heat, dust and eventual cold. With the oil fires burning, the dog's form soaked into the marble tiles, where its horrified owners found it when they were eventually able to return to Kuwait. When it was lifted away, the carcass, mere skin and bone, left behind the dog's outline — a sad reminder of the horrors that had overtaken it. The family still cannot bear to have any pets.

The story of the zoo llama and two Syrian bears had a somewhat more cheerful ending. Three young Kuwaitis managed to get into the zoo and each took one animal with them back to their house. One young man was asked how on earth he had managed to keep a large bear alive and he said cheerfully that whatever he had to eat, a roll of bread, some rice, it was a case of 'half for me and half for you'. The three animals have now been handed back to the zoo. A number of Kuwaitis tried to help the zoo animals by going in, for at least as long as they could, to feed the animals on any suitable leftovers they had been able to find. The zoo animals were badly treated by the soldiers who shot at them, on occasions ate them and never attempted to feed or water them.

September began with a mass protest. Through telephone calls and circulars secretly distributed by the Resistance, it was arranged that everyone would climb onto the top of their roofs at midnight and, as loudly as possible, would shout their defiance and fury at what had taken place — at the invasion, the brutality that had followed, the killings, and the torture centres that had been set up in various places around Kuwait. As a further show of indignation nobody would go outside their houses at all the next day, thus leaving the Iraqis in no doubt at all about what the population felt. Not that they could be harbouring many illusions from the amount of resistance, from both men and women, there had been over the past month. A rumour circulated in our district that a satellite would be passing over Kuwait at midnight and would capture everyone on top of their roofs shouting defiance at the Iraqis.

At 10 minutes before midnight we climbed up the stairs and made our way to the rooftop, where we stood near the railings looking at our watches and waiting for the hour to strike. As our rooftop is quite a high one it was possible to see all the other men, women and children moving round on their roofs. At 12.00 on the dot a huge uproar broke out, rolling in waves through the still hot air — *"Ilah-u-Akbar'*, *'Allah-u-Akbar'* (God is Great).

Around and around rolled the voices of men, women and children, as they cried out their plea for help and their rejection and defiance of the brutal intruders. In the middle of the rooftop demonstration a sudden sharp sustained fusillade of shots rang out. Alarmed Iraqis were trying to quieten the noise. We heard that in some districts militiamen had fired their guns directly at houses where they could see people shouting. There was silence for the space of an indrawn breath and then the shouts broke out with renewed vigour. Our voices became hoarse and strained. One or two people appeared to have loudspeakers and the roars of the defiance continued. For an hour, from midnight until about 1.00 a.m., all over Kuwait the awesome sounds continued. It was an emotional experience. It brought back the horror of what had happened and the despair one felt, yet, through it all, one could sense a steely communal determination to continue to brave the Iraqis. The soldiers, no doubt upset and put out by this amazing show of defiance, shot more warning rounds. Gradually the sounds of the demonstration died away and people slowly came down from their roofs to go off to their uncomfortable sleep.

The next morning, there was an even more deathly hush than usual in our area as, to hammer the point home further, no one ventured out of their houses. Even the small boys and girls kept within their garden walls. One of the most noticeable changes since the invasion had been the fall in the amount of traffic other than trailers and military vehicles. Some form of transport was necessary for getting around Kuwait, but with so many vehicles being stolen and road checks everywhere, people had taken to using their oldest, most battered car for going out and looking for food. Because it was often so dangerous for men to be outdoors, the women tended to be the ones to hunt down food at the various street markets. When some Kuwaiti women, mainly widows of soldiers killed at the beginning of the invasion, had been seen hunting for scraps in the rubbish, a system for distribution to the needy was organized. Women prepared and packed up food parcels and then drove out to distribute them where they might be needed. It was dangerous work because of the many army checks. If caught, at best the food would be removed; but it was quite possible the driver might be beaten or taken to prison.

Sitting indoors watching television we saw some of the women and children who had been in hiding arriving at Heathrow. Most of them had strained faces, for many had left their husbands behind in Kuwait and were wary of saying anything that might indicate where their husbands might be staying. Some women had had their identity cards taken away by the Iraqis, who, noting that these cards contained street addresses, had immediately surrounded the house in question and arrested the husband. On the news it was announced that Iraq wished to link talks about Palestine and the West Bank to the situation in Kuwait. But, as the UN secretary-general, Javier Pérez de Cuéllar, was to remark at his press interview about this sudden notion, 'One sin should not inspire another.' I glanced out through the window and saw a big army lorry filled with rifle-toting soldiers come lurching over the sand, past the spreading, half burned rubbish tip.

It trundled slowly across and over the kerb onto the road. The men in it were Red Beret Republican Guards, the professional soldiers of Iraq. They stared with interest at the houses, as if wondering what was in them and what they could plan to take. The truck moved on down the road, but a little later on it reappeared, this time moving forward at a crawl. As it came alongside our house the lorry faltered and for a heart-stopping moment I thought it was our turn for a house search. It was the first of many such occasions. I rang Keaton next door, but he had seen them and was preparing to hide immediately as far back in the air-conditioning ducts as he could get. His wife (who was Singaporean), their children and the two Filipinas were there as well and, in theory at least, did not have to hide. Dressed up in *abat* and headscarves, they were all ready to open the door, for if they did not, the army would simply kick it in and probably rampage through the house. Nadr and Abu Ali (if he were around at the time) would then go over and, hopefully, the presence of two men might act as a brake on any base ideas the soldiers might have had in a house full of women and children.

My friend and school colleague, Gladys, who is Indian, was hiding one of our British teachers from school. As the army lorry was crawling past our house, she rang to say that Janet had suffered a painful gall bladder attack the previous evening, which had been so bad that she had taken her to a private hospital not far down the road from us. With government clinics and hospitals now completely out of bounds, they had had to risk numerous road checks to get her to the clinic. As a precaution, Janet had dyed her blond hair black and they managed to arrive unseen. All hospitals, private and government, were forbidden to treat westerners and had been instructed to turn in any who wanted treatment. Though staff at the Al Hadi Hospital felt unable to keep Janet, they did at least put her on a drip for a short time and provide her with various pills and painkillers before the two women made their dangerous way back to their flat. Upstairs in one of the private rooms of the hospital, also in hiding, was an American recovering from a heart operation, who for the first week of the invasion did not know what had happened. Like Janet, he and his wife eventually managed to get onto the list of people with medical problems and they were airlifted out of Kuwait via Baghdad.

As I put down the phone, it immediately rang again and Mr Khan from the flats, speaking rapidly in a low voice, said that there had been a mysterious phone call to his flat warning him that it was known he was hiding British people and that if he kept them there the Iraqis would be informed. He was told to get rid of them as soon as possible or he and his family would suffer the consequences. It seemed obvious that someone had seen Bill and Kate arriving two weeks before and realized they were westerners.

Once again my mind clicked over trying to think of somewhere 'safe', at least for a day or two. The school was now thoroughly unsafe, although Abu Yaseen and a couple of guards were attempting to guard it. Soldiers had been inside at least twice and one of the commanders had taken to turning up every day and demanding that tea be made for him. On one recent occasion he had kicked open the locked secondary school office, stared around at the computers and office equipment, and repeated his previous accusation that 'this is no school, but more like a spy centre'. He constantly asked where 'the Kuwaiti lackey of the British, Tareq Sayid' was. Even considering the possibility of running a few quiet classes for children, let alone hiding anyone in there, was out of the question. The director's house was being watched and occasionally being looted from the nearby government school, although one of our maintenance staff was still staying in one of the outhouses in the director's compound.

We decided that it was imperative to go over to the flats and collect Bill and Kate as soon as possible. They could stay with Keaton for the time being. While making arrangements with the warden for Janet to leave Kuwait (it was with much reluctance that she decided to go), Gladys had also discussed Kate and Bill's situation.

Nadr backed out the small, slightly rattly Suzuki, which, on account of its age, had so far escaped the attentions of the Iraqis. I handed him a bag containing an *abaya*, as well as a man's *dishdasha* and white *kuffiyer* for Bill, and he clattered off through the side roads and over pavements to fetch them. As he approached the flats, he realized that a thousand unfriendly eyes might be watching everything, just as we now were, and that they could all be caught in the act of escaping. Quickly Bill and Kate put on their disguises and, as unobtrusively as possible, slipped into the car, Bill once more being trampled underfoot in the back. They set off down the side roads, hoping to avoid any sudden road checks. I hovered near the gates to let them through and into the house before any army or foot soldiers saw them. Their faces strained and grey (for by now Kate and Bill had had at least four moves, each time just ahead of being caught by the army), they rushed through the door and upstairs. There we collapsed at the table by the window and drank soothing cups of tea. It was rather stewed tea, for that was now in short supply and I had developed the habit of placing a pot on a very low fire and reusing tea bags. Somehow throughout the entire time we always had tea available to perform its calming job!

As we sat exchanging our experiences, the telephone rang once again. It was one of the wardens, Mike Devey, saying that a bus had been organized for women, children and sick people. It would leave for Baghdad at 6.00 a.m. the next day from the Sultan Centre car park, which was well known by practically everyone. Keaton's wife and children and Kate were strongly advised to leave as no one had much idea of what turn events were going to take. None of them wanted to go, but Jinn had the children to consider and another place had to be found for Bill. It was therefore thought that Kate should take the opportunity to go as well. Kate had previously hidden her jalopy down the side path of a friend's house not too far away from us and Bill and Nadr went off, Bill still in his *dishdasha*, to try and collect it. Everyone had to find their own way to the Sultan Centre car park as it was impossible to organize transport when people lived all over Kuwait. The question was would they be allowed through the roadblocks? In theory the Iraqis were now permitting women and children to go by bus to Iraq, do the deliberately nonsensical paperwork required in Baghdad and then get on planes for Amman in Jordan. From there they would be able to fly out to Britain, the US and elsewhere. But events were moving so fast and the Iraqis were so unreliable that one never knew how the 'rules' would change from day to day. There was also the worry that the Iraqis were well aware that the women must have come from buildings in which their husbands were hiding. Keaton tutored Jinn and Kate on how to avoid giving information during any question sessions they might have to face.

When evening came and darkness had fallen we all went over to Keaton to find Jinn looking worried and upset. Her small daughter, Melissa, had developed a fever and it was uncertain whether she would be able to travel. Nadr and I went slowly back to our place next door, afraid to stay away too long for, although searches generally seemed to take place during the daylight hours, we had heard that that was by no means the rule.

Kate, Jinn and the two small children set off by car in the early hours of the morning to reach the meeting place. They tried to avoid roadblocks, but they were amongst the 57 women and children who were stopped. They were waved through at least three checks with no problems, but at the last one the soldiers did not seem to have heard that women and children had been allowed to leave. They protested, argued and complained but were not allowed to continue and were arrested. Typically, it seemed that most but not all the Iraqi soldiers had been given orders to allow women, children and the sick through to the Sultan Centre. Or it might have been that just to make things difficult the authorities had decided to stop a few people as an example of the mental torture the regime knew so well how to apply.

None of us knew what had happened and we were all on edge wondering what had befallen the party. Eventually Kate managed to ring up from a hotel to tell us that, along with others, they had been 'caught' and taken to the Meridien Hotel, which was the hotel at which Keaton had been general manager. In a way this was unfortunate because Jinn knew everybody working there. Two months before the invasion the hotel had hired an Iraqi from Baghdad who had now taken over as general manager and it was essential that Jinn not be seen by him. Fortunately slightly later on they were all removed to the Regency Palace Hotel, where no one would know who Jinn was.

Although they had been told not to do so, three men travelled along with the women and children. On that same occasion, I believe, one of them had tried to pass himself off as a woman and a 19-year-old had been told he could not be considered a child. An 11-week-old baby was suffering from heat exhaustion, for everyone had been left standing out in the hot sun while the Iraqis had looked for transport. As I talked to Kate, I could hear more sounds of heavy shooting and clouds of smoke appeared down the road from the direction of the hospital. In the end Kate, Jinn and the two children did manage to leave and get back to England and Singapore respectively. All of us watched the arrivals of women and children on television, hoping against hope that we might see Kate, Jinn and the children. But for some time there was no news at all. Then I caught a brief glimpse of Keaton's little daughter Melissa sitting on top of a pile of baggage in an airport lounge and looking perfectly calm and collected.

6

Terror Tactics and Outrageous Orders

THE politicians and world leaders batted the political ball back and forth across the net. Saddam made more grandiloquent speeches and did what he was good at, which was employing delaying tactics. Cunningly he now tried to inspire the Arab world into declaring a Holy War or *jihad* against the 'infidels' and Iraqi TV started to show more shots of Saddam at prayer. One particularly irritating and much-used still showed him from the waist up, his hands upheld in the normally beautiful attitude of prayer. It was hard to believe that some saw him as an ardent Arab and devout Muslim. Indeed the harm he had inflicted on the Arab and Islamic world made one wonder just whose side he was on.

It can hardly be said that the people of Kuwait had adjusted to their new life. They just survived and there was still an element of 'if Iraq has nearly looted everything, perhaps it will then retreat from Kuwait'. Having discovered that there was absolutely no popular support for the invasion or their presence, the Iraqis fast introduced terror tactics to subdue the Kuwaiti population. Pictures in ceramics and photographs of Saddam in his favourite Austrian hat, as Saladin on a white horse, in one of his many self-awarded uniforms, or in his Arab sheikh guise had been pasted onto every roundabout, wall, school and lamppost. All we could think of was how much we would like to shoot these photographs to pieces. In Rumaithiya, the district next to us, where many Kuwaitis were living, the Resistance continued to put up Kuwaiti flags and posters of the Amir. They were slung across the road and round the lampposts. Daily they were torn or shot down by the Iraqis and replaced with pro-Saddam banners. We muttered ominously but were unable to do anything publicly. The 'sin' of even a minor criticism of Saddam was viewed very seriously and certain death followed.

One morning Rowa went with a group of her friends to get their ration of bread from the co-op; they parked their car near an army truck filled with bread removed from the supermarket. Nadia, always a person given to speaking her mind bluntly, shouted out to the soldier guarding it: 'Where did you get that bread?'

'I bought it.'

'Stole it you mean,' replied Nadia.

Looking indignant, even though lying through his teeth, 'Didn't, I paid for it.'

'You took it, stole it, just as you did Kuwait,' snapped back Nadia.

Her friends by now were looking a little alarmed and trying to move her on.

'I didn't, I didn't, I swear by the Holy Kaaba, I didn't.'

She replied tartly, 'What do you mean? You don't know what Islam is, let alone what the Holy Kaaba is.'

At this the soldier looked very indignant, and twiddled his rifle around replying, 'What *do* you mean? I'm a Muslim.'

Here Nadia really became upset and spat out, '*Muslim* — you? Of course you are not. You stole Kuwait. Which hell will you go to?'

Smugly the man answered, 'Not to hell, but to Saddam's heaven.'

At which point, while Nadia gaped in disbelief and annoyance, the others dragged her muttering off to the now three-quarters empty shelved market.

Although it was risky speaking to soldiers in this manner, people sometimes did as Nadia had done out of sheer fury and frustration. And they sometimes got away with it, as in the case of the man on the tank at the women's demonstration, who rattled his gun but was not yet incensed enough to do more. But once they were in groups, like packs of dogs they easily turned vicious. For example, a Pakistani who had decided to go and stay with relatives because he was alone in the area, had just packed his bag, brushed his hair and was about to leave his flat when suddenly the door was kicked in and soldiers poured into the room. Advancing on him they asked him his nationality and on finding out that he was a Pakistani, they all picked up pieces of piping and beat him severely. There was little to steal and after a while, tiring of the fun, they left. Slowly and painfully dragging himself off the floor and already swollen all over, he managed to make his way to his relative's house and eventually succeeded in leaving Kuwait.

On and around 12 September people going into the cooperatives (government supported supermarkets in which the residents of the district own shares) were handed a news-sheet by the Iraqi *Mubahath* (intelligence) on which various orders that had to be complied with within the next few days were printed. There were always armed soldiers and intelligence men in and around the cooperatives and everyone had to show their identity card as they entered. Eventually, as food became harder to obtain, one could only go to the one in the district in which one lived. Amongst the orders on the news-sheet everyone had been made to take were the following instructions to the general population:

Kuwaitis should surrender any weapons they had and those who refused to do so were liable to be executed.

Any house from which shots were fired would be demolished, as well as any houses that happened to be nearby.

Civil servants failing to report for duty would be sacked in accordance with a Revolution Command Council instruction. (Most people were already 'sacked' as only those in essential services were allowed to stay at work.)

And, most alarming of all and causing considerable fear, was the stipulation that:

All Kuwaitis must take their vehicles to the Basra Traffic Department for new numberplates or their cars would be confiscated.

The new, badly produced numberplates were made with the number on top and below the words 'El Iraq/Kuwait'. In Arabic this meant the country was Iraq, while Kuwait was just a town belonging to it. Thousands of cars, vans and lorries from Kuwait streamed into Jordan where these new number plates were legal. But only cars with their original Kuwaiti numberplates were allowed to enter Syria, Egypt and Lebanon.

The warden had now arranged a suitable hideout for Bill and, after much sometimes cryptic discussion over the telephone, we thought we understood where the new flat might be located. It seemed to be quite close to our house. There must have been hundreds of people in hiding in Jabriya and I suspect that practically every road housed at least one or two of them. Once, while I was walking down some nearby streets, I caught a glimpse of some bare white legs through a gate. Someone was watering the garden and as I came unexpectedly round the corner, the person, who must have caught sight of me, dropped the hose and rapidly disappeared indoors. It was most likely someone in hiding. Some Kuwaitis lived in the house next door to him and on other occasions I saw them going through the front gate with plates of food. Hidden down at the side of the house was a car that had originally had diplomatic numberplates, but which now had none at all. Within the next couple of days the gate was boarded over and it became impossible to glance through and see anything.

I drew a careful map of the new hideaway and we decided that when it became dark it would be safer and easier for the three of us to walk to it. Nadr would then drop Bill's suitcase over a little later. Alas! I was not at all a suitable candidate for the secret service. We walked across the sand, careful to keep a lookout for army jeeps or wandering soldiers. Past the building where everyone, soldiers included, was standing in a fairly orderly queue to buy what little bread they were allowed. Nervously, for the main road we came out onto was alive with the army walking back and forth from the government school they had taken over. During the periods that it was possible to take a walk I used to pass by that school as far on the other side of the road as I could for there were always bored army faces looking out of the smashed-in windows. We turned the corner and went down into the side streets and tried to find the distinguishing signs that were supposed to tell us we had come to the correct building. Nothing was right at all. We wandered up and down and to anyone who might be watching, we began to look suspicious and obvious characters. It was clearly dangerous to keep walking up and down the road, and the whole thing was taking on an air of farce. In spite of my maps and what I had thought was an easy building to find, it seemed many buildings could fit the 'past the blue mosque, turn to the right and—' description. We trailed back home, somewhat dispirited and slightly giggly, and began all over again.

This time we got it right. The flats were in quite the opposite direction, but as they too were seething with soldiers Nadr decided to drive Bill there in the Suzuki. A Filipino man was waiting discreetly by the gate to open it and let him slip in to settle down in his new 'home'. At the end of the road was a recently completed white painted house belonging to a member of the Al Sabah family. It was a pleasant Arab-style structure with a palm filled garden and had been just about ready to move into. Bill and the other two men he joined in hiding watched it being officially looted from their window. The army drew up with its trailers and everything from the house was thrown in and carried away. Much later on what we supposed to be an important army commander occupied the house for a while. There was heavy security and both ends of the road were sealed off while he was there, then once again it became empty and open to the wind, with doors flapping on their hinges and the windows smashed. Just outside on the corner of the road a small street market grew up. As petrol became scarce, the sellers would bring their cars, park them on the sand behind and spend the daylight hours selling whatever they could. Food was everybody's early and ever worsening worry.

Once a soldier stood on that corner holding up for sale three little hotel bottles of jam, which must have been stolen. Dead soldiers were quite often found in the area near the white house, presumably killed at night by the Resistance, or even perhaps by individuals. The road would then be blocked off at both ends and the buildings in the vicinity would once again be searched. When the Iraqis left Kuwait they planted small explosives in the earth of the flower pots in the garden, causing one unfortunate man to lose his fingers when he tried, after liberation, to tidy up the grounds.

7

House to House Searches and Fire Bombing

ONE morning as I was writing my journal, Mr Khan rang to say that quite a number of people had been 'picked up' from the surrounding flats and taken away by the Iraqis. He thought that the men taken were Europeans. Presumably they had become part of the 'human shield'. Looking back to that particular Friday, I find that I wrote in my journal:

> While we all like to imagine or think that the Iraqis are removing everything they can lay hands on and will then leave like the locusts they are, I have been having far more horrible ideas about their plans. So horrible that I am not even going to write them down. And while I am on about horrible thoughts, Nadr says that the Science College in the university complex is now being used as a place of torture.

We were to find out later that this was true.

Nadr had gone off to his uncle's house to see how they were managing and on the road just before their house had run into a *tefteesh* (road inspection). He presented his ID; the *jindi* glanced at it and handed it back. As Nadr pressed his foot on the accelerator and took back the card, by mistake his hand brushed against the man's rifle, which was carelessly resting on the open window, and knocked it against the man's chest. Nadr's heart sank and, as he opened his mouth, the soldier for some reason began to apologize, 'It was a mistake.... I didn't mean to.... I'm so sorry.' He was still saying sorry as Nadr put his foot on the accelerator and moved thankfully away.

About a quarter of a mile down the road from our house were two adjoining villas, which my husband had built and eventually sold to two Kuwaiti brothers and their families. One Saturday, just before midday prayer time, my brother-in-law Abu Fakhry arrived with some food cooked by his wife. As usual we sat at the table near the window and embarked on all anybody ever talked about these days, cursing the Iraqis and discussing the latest happenings. Eventually we went downstairs into the sunshine and suddenly, very close to us, there was a deafening boom, followed by the rattle of gunfire and salvos of small explosions. Clouds of thick black smoke began to drift over us and the smell and crackle of burning could be felt and heard. Jeeps and soldiers began to converge from all directions, and through the smoke I realized it was the brothers' two houses that were burning fiercely. There were shots everywhere, but coming particularly from the direction of the houses. I could see soldiers running round the back, but because of the way the houses faced I could not see exactly what was happening. I rushed upstairs to try and find my camera, but because we were expecting house searches I had hidden it so well that it was another three weeks before I was able to find it again. There were loud splintering cracks as windows exploded, and cars tore aimlessly about on the sand. The people inside the mosque must have wondered what more was happening.

Properties very near to the two houses were in imminent danger of also catching alight. So ferociously did the fire rage that it seemed entirely possible we might all become part of the conflagration. About one and a half hours later the fire engines began to arrive, as well as an ambulance. By then the men had come out of the mosque and they stood around watching. Nadr went out to join them. One of the Kuwaiti firemen muttered to him that the house had been purposely RPGd (rocket-propelled grenaded) as the owners were both Kuwait Army men and suspected of being in the Resistance. They had to stop talking, for the Iraqis watched the Kuwaiti firefighters very closely and if they put one step wrong they would be imprisoned or worse. The owners had indeed been in the Resistance and there had probably been ammunition hidden there as well. The Iraqi Army had turned up, surrounded the houses and started the fire by slamming RPGs into it.

The houses burned ferociously and then steamed and smoked for nearly three days before they were finally completely gutted. The family, the Deshtis, had all been involved in the Resistance and, by the end, had lost 37 members as either prisoners or fighters — not an easy thing to accept or forgive. The family still has two of its members in Iraqi prisons as POWs.

What I feared had now begun to happen. Abu Yaseen rang from the school to say that trucks and jeeps had once more arrived there and would be coming back for 'it belongs to the state'. Both Mr Khan and Mohammed Sofdar, our secondary school secretary, had been in their offices at the time and had been subjected to a battery of questions. A great deal of interest had been shown not only in the buses, but also (and particularly) in the new pick-up, or wanette. The wanette had attracted their attention before. A soldier had attempted to get it started, but having failed did the usual thing of pulling out whatever wires he could and kicking in one of the windows. There was now little pretence of law when stealing cars. The soldiery would order people out, even if their papers were correct, and tell them to go to the local police station to claim back their vehicle. Needless to say, the police at the station would deny any knowledge of the car and nothing further could be done.

It appeared that the takeover of the school was imminent, for lorry loads of army men kept coming and going, then getting out and looking around it. At the same time as the school was being commandeered, rumours about water from the distillation plant were circulating all over Kuwait. One held that chemicals for purifying water had nearly run out; another that poison was going to be introduced into the supply and piped along to kill us all. While these were in fact no more than rumours, they caused the population considerable anxiety and may have been put around for that purpose. Kuwaiti and other engineers struggled very hard to keep water supplies running despite the shortages of staff and materials. There was a real fear, of course, that it would be cut off entirely. Plants and trees were dying in empty houses and along the roads and, for well over a month now, Kuwait had hardly been cleaned, least of all by the Iraqis who had done nothing whatsoever to retain any of the public facilities.

Although there was no guarantee that house searches took place only in the daytime — in fact they were just as likely to happen in the middle of the night — I was somehow never bothered by the thought of night searches. But I was nevertheless unable to remain in bed any later than about 5.45 a.m. Every day I would wake at 5.00, though for the first time in my life groaning at the thought of yet another day, then firmly close my eyes to try and sleep for a little longer, but was never able to do so. I always left the window slightly open so that I would be able to hear anything unusual. Gunshots and explosions were no longer unusual, or even particularly worrying, but one's mind nonetheless registered the sounds and automatically tried to interpret them and find an explanation for what might have caused them.

By now I had a set routine. I would leap out of bed and go straight to the window to look for signs of the army before proceeding to every other window in turn to check for suspicious movements. Occasionally a couple of soldiers would walk by with their rifles over their shoulders, probably to queue for their rations of bread at the bakery. Few if any professional bakers were left in Kuwait and, while flour supplies lasted, young Kuwaitis regularly went in to make the bread. A great deal of flour had already been taken out of storage and sent off to Iraq, but for the first few weeks the usual white flaps of bread known as *khubiz Libnani* (Lebanese bread) had been available. All the other kinds, including the thin delicious *khubiz Irani* (Iranian bread), which had been a speciality of the Iranian bakers, were no longer being made.

As time went on the bread turned from white to sandy beige, to pale brown and on to a dark gritty colour before the flour ran out altogether. While the peace activists were calling for one more chance for 'peace', the people of Kuwait were each allowed five small flaps of bread a day, then there were queues at the main bakery once or twice a week — queues that curled like some grey fearsome snake round and round and round the block again. In the end there was no bread at all. Those who were lucky and had some flour made their own bread and gave what they could to any neighbours who had none left and many children to feed. Some entrepreneurs even contrived, with the aid of a gas ring and tin barrel, to sell a 'fire' that could be used for baking thin bread on its walls.

One morning I awoke even earlier and more uneasy than usual. Having been up all night, Nadr had just gone to sleep after drinking a cup of tea. I peered through the windows and then reluctantly removed a small Kuwaiti flag and little doll dressed in Kuwaiti colours I had left sitting defiantly on a shelf. Suddenly through the kitchen window, in the direction of the French and Chinese embassies, I saw soldiers, too many of them for that time of morning. Very uneasily I went to the other windows and, seeing nothing unusual, finally went to the window that looked out to the houses behind us and towards the school. To my horror I saw the red berets of the Republican Guards, one standing with his rifle outside a block of flats. Rushing back to my bedroom window I peered outside as far as I could and there were army buses arriving and parking outside. They disgorged men all holding rifles who fanned out in different directions towards the houses on the other side of the sand and in the roads all around us. This had to be a house-to-house search. As I grabbed the phone by the kitchen window a wanette, with a machine gun mounted on its roof and loaded with rifle-toting soldiers, drew up alongside our wall.

After waking Nadr, who having only just gone to sleep looked dazed for a moment or two before understanding what was happening, I dialled Keaton next door. He never picked up the telephone on the grounds that if the lines were tapped and an obviously English speaking male voice was heard answering, it would be easy to locate the house and go in and arrest him. We had discussed what to do in the event of a house search and had arranged that the Filipina, Nita, would always answer the phone. I would tell her that 'soldiers are here Nita' and she would say 'yes' and then, having put it down, would immediately go and warn Keaton, who would then go and hide in the air-conditioning ducts. There was no reason why she should not be there and Jinn and the children had already left Kuwait.

She answered after a ring or two and I twice slowly and clearly said 'Soldiers are here Nita, do you understand?' and she replied 'Yes.' Then, banging down the phone, I rushed off to get dressed at top speed. Putting on my headscarf and *abaya*, I tried to decide what kind of expression one wore for an occasion of this kind. My mouth was dry and I dropped everything I picked up. Then Nadr and I rushed back to the kitchen window. They were moving across the sand and into both occupied and empty houses and everyone must have been in the same state of jumpy nervousness as we were. From what I could see, the houses directly behind us were in the midst of a house-by-house, door-by-door search. I later found out that people in a couple of

91

the houses near us had been directly involved in the Resistance and that stocks of arms and ammunition had been placed under the floor of a sitting room. The women all sat in that room while the head of the household politely went out to meet the officer in charge of the group. He conducted them through the house, mentioning that the women were all together in that room and urging him to move past it without looking too closely. Under normal circumstances, it is considered impolite in this part of the world to inspect women's quarters too closely and on this occasion it worked. Eventually, after a cursory glance around, the army moved out and on to the next houses — there were an awful lot of houses to look at and, as is common in countries with hot climates, many of them were rather large.

Across the sand we could see that they had entered an empty house in which only a guard had been living. Through its garden gates jerked an automatic BMW. An officer, who had obviously demanded the ignition key and started the engine, was now kangaroo hopping over the road, crashing up the pavement and across the sand. He had clearly not driven an automatic before and, much to the amusement of the other men, he continued to kick up the sand until the car shot out onto the road and jerked to a stop outside our front gate. Try as the man would, the car was stuck and a group gathered around it to peer inside and to pocket some of the music tapes in the glove compartment. Eventually someone did get it started and it was driven away, never to be seen again. Some days earlier another car had for some reason broken down while being driven into hiding and had been left standing on the sand. Now the soldiers were hovering round it like flies. They tried to open a door, they fiddled with the boot and a few of them started rocking it from side to side. Tiring of this game, one of them suddenly aimed a karate-type kick at the window on the driver's side; the pane cracked and splintered with a loud pop. The door was opened and they tried to start the engine. When this failed they proceeded to pull out all the wires they could find, puncture one of the tyres and, after a struggle, to open the bonnet. They then pulled out all the removable bits of the engine and threw them over their shoulders.

With my stomach sinking and knowing there was no further time or point in going once again to the bathroom, it was our turn: the army was congregating outside. Nadr began to go downstairs to the front gate and coming out from the flat below was his brother-in-law. They arrived together as the officer pushed his way through. The Saluki (a desert hunting dog) was barking hysterically, but fortunately was separated from the passage by a wooden fence. He stood in danger of being shot outright. A few days before a friend's dog had been outside their house when the soldiers arrived and, as dogs will, had begun to bark. And, even though he had not been attacking — in fact he had kept well away but just barked — he was simply shot through the head. As the soldiers all began to troop upstairs I saw one at the tail end come through the door and this set off another round of the dog leaping up and down and barking. Startled, the man fell through the door, recovered himself and came towards the Saluki, pointing his rifle at him, which merely encouraged a worse outburst. Shaking his head and tut-tutting, the man followed the rest upstairs and I went and positioned myself just inside the sitting area.

The officer entered first, followed by Nadr, my son-in-law and soldiers, who fanned out to pull open drawers and cupboards. One or two stopped and stood staring at the indoor garden. The officer stamped to a halt, looked towards Nadr with a wide smile and said grandly, 'We've come to give you your freedom.'

My jaw fell. Should I laugh outright at this? Could I manage to look polite? Should I mutter a meaningless form of agreement? Should I smile politely? God damn him and all his lot is what I really thought.

Fortunately he did nothing more than glance in my direction and went round into the various rooms, opening a cupboard, rummaging a bit and closing it. I had hidden quite a few Kuwaiti flags and posters around the house, but they would only come to light in a really determined search. After what seem ages they began to move off towards the house next door. I was ordered to stay where I was and my stomach turned over several times more. I could hear them all talking as they went downstairs, out into the road and then along the side of the house as our main door was being locked, bolted and having something jammed up against it. All the cars were covered and could not be seen easily. As they reached the door of the next house and Nita opened it, Nadr stood slightly blocking the opening and talking as loudly in Arabic as he could. He must have had a premonition for he did it to give Keaton as much time as possible, just in case the message had not got through to him.

They stepped into the house, Nita disappeared, obviously panic-stricken, and slowly the army began to go into the various rooms, opening cupboard doors, sliding aside a pair of trousers, peering into the drawer underneath. Upstairs, although I had packed away nearly everything, I had forgotten a photograph taken a year before of my older son Ziad in his conscript's army uniform. The officer picked it up, stared at it, removed it from the frame and tore it in half remarking, 'It is illegal to have photographs of people in uniform. If there are any more tear them up and throw them away.' It was apparently illegal to possess any kind of army, navy or air force uniform and I had completely forgotten that Ziad had some in his cupboard, which fortunately were not noticed. Later on we found the rubbish tips full of uniforms thrown there after it was learned that one could easily be shot for having them.

Meanwhile, I was standing near the window after having watched everyone go next door. In my mind I could hear the shots if Keaton were to be discovered and I nearly jumped out of my skin when the phone shrilled in the other room. It was an acquaintance in hiding, who was surrounded by the army, though not actually involved in a search at that point. After that the phone rang occasionally to say that the Jabriya area had been sealed off while the searches were conducted, as had another area with a large Kuwaiti population, Khaitan. We had some relatives living there and I wondered how they were doing.

There was no sound from next door, but it was too risky to sneak downstairs to try and find out what was happening because the soldiers were standing around on guard outside with their rifles at the ready. Others were still wandering around with whatever they had picked up from the houses they had entered.

A door slammed and Nadr and Ghazi, followed by the officer and the rifle-carrying soldiers, appeared from the side of the house, Nadr looking a trifle pale but otherwise normal. There had been no shots and it appeared that everything had gone well. The officer and his troop went off down the road to carry on with their house searches. I ran down the steps to go and see what had happened and, just as the two men were entering the front door, a completely different officer strode up and demanded to conduct a search. He was a nasty-looking somewhat sour-faced character and it was obvious he was itching to get inside the house and see what was there. Nadr and Ghazi glared at him and retorted that the house had only just been searched and cleared, so what was the point of another one? Threateningly, his mouth stretched in a thin mean line, he ordered them to stand aside and the soldiers behind began to move forward. This search would be a far more thorough, careful one and I could envisage our flags, pictures, cameras and everything else being tossed out of the cupboard or stolen and then all of us being shot or, even worse, taken away to be hanged. As we turned to go upstairs, the original officer appeared from down the road, marched up to the man and asked what he was doing; the three houses standing in a row had already been searched by himself and it was unnecessary to do them again. There were plenty more to get done before their duty was over. Fortunately for us the second officer was lower in rank and, scowling but unable to say anything to his superior, he grudgingly moved away and out of sight.

The searches that day continued for about six hours before the trucks and their occupants began to move away and out of the district. It was only later when everything was quiet that we went next door to find out if Keaton had come down out of the air-conditioning ducts. He had heard the telephone ringing in the early morning and shouted out to Nita to find out what the call was about. She had not replied. Keaton had taken to sleeping on a mattress at the back of a raised loft instead of in the bed in the room. He had been afraid that if the Iraqis arrived unexpectedly he would be unable to move quickly enough through the hatch and into the ducts. Thinking that the telephone call had just been another of the slightly suspicious ones everyone received, and which we suspected were the *Mukhabarat* checking on people in houses, he had gone back to sleep.

About half an hour later he woke once more to hear men speaking Arabic inside the house. He froze where he lay as the door of the room beneath him was pushed open and men with rifles came in. Fortunately they did not look up at the loft. When they left the room, he crawled through the hatch and along for about 50 feet to the far end of the air-conditioning duct. There he waited for about four hours, unable to tell whether or not they had gone. Then, when Nita happened to come within a few feet of the ventilation grating, he whispered, 'Have they left yet?' Receiving a reply in the affirmative, he slithered back along the ducts, through the hatch and lowered the stepladder back down onto the floor. Apparently Nita had completely misunderstood the message and had gone off to make tea for visitors! When she opened the door to see Nadr with all the armed soldiers behind him, she had understandably panicked, fled and hidden herself somewhere in the house.

Nearly everybody had stories to tell about house searches, some of which ended in people being shot and left dead or dying on their doorsteps. Some people were not searched at all, though they tended to be in the minority. A married couple with children at university in the United States (acquaintances who were probably being searched at the same time as we were, for they lived nearby) found their house suddenly surrounded by the army, so the owner went downstairs to let them in. On spotting a small safe in the couple's bedroom and knowing that it more than likely contained jewellery and perhaps some money, the officer in charge held a gun to the wife's head, demanded the key to the safe and then locked the couple in another room, where they remained for the next six hours listening to the sound of heavy boots tramping all over their house and the occasional smash as plates fell to the floor. When the house finally fell and remained silent, the husband began to try to get the door unlocked. When he eventually got it open, they found the empty safe lying on its side, the house in a terrible mess and everything of value removed.

One disaster always seems to be followed by another and, shortly after the house searches, the Iraqi Army requisitioned the school as a barracks. The new half-completed teachers' flats had nearly everything removed from them apart from some iron bars and a few bags of cement. The site manager's Portakabin, along with its photocopier, water coolers, chairs and tables, was completely wrecked, with the door and windows left hanging crazily off their hinges. Most of the flats had been ransacked and, reluctant to remain at the mercy of passing soldiers, any residents that had been there had left — an eerie atmosphere hung over the area. As the site had not yet been completely developed, there were wide open spaces surrounding it, which rapidly became marshy if heavy rain fell. Later on the Iraqis began to prepare themselves for the expected Allied seaborne landings by digging some basic underground bunkers there, but probably did not realize what a heavy rainfall would do to them.

Out in the desert amongst the ordinary sandbag-lined bunkers were large marble-lined bunkers, presumably built for the visits of very important officials. Inside one of them mine clearers found some of the special government crockery used at official banquets. The marble had been taken from marble factories in Kuwait and most found its way to Baghdad and reputedly Jordan. The bunkers near the flats were good enough while the weather remained dry, but once rain fell the ground rapidly became a sludgy mass of puddles that turned into lakes. Eventually the place could be smelt a mile away, for there were hundreds of soldiers dug in and it became impossible any longer to go and see what was happening to the building site.

Towards the end of September we all started to follow a certain grim routine. At night Nadr kept watch and, hidden away behind the costume cupboards in the exhibition area, worked on his computer. The walls of this room were covered in a plain material suitable for exhibitions. Its layout was such that it was hard to tell that behind the walls there were drawers and cupboards for textiles and a tiny room into which the computer and various other bits of machinery were crammed. I tried again to work on some cataloguing, but that proved impossible: the threat of searches, of possibly being arrested, was always there. Keaton kept watch from his side and I looked out of the window from my side. If I went shopping, Nadr kept watch. One day he saw the Suzuki, which was parked outside, being surrounded by soldiers. He rushed downstairs and said harshly to them, 'What are you doing?' It was always better to adopt a confident attitude: like packs of dogs they could relate only to strong language.

'We're looking for a stolen Suzuki,' replied one, trying to appear official. Then he added, 'Are there many like this type?'

'Thousands,' answered Nadr, 'and this one is not stolen.'

After a short discussion about the no doubt fictitious stolen Suzuki the soldiers drifted off down the road.

8

Living under the Yoke of Oppression

Eaarly in October the Iraqis issued another order. This time all identity cards (as well as car numberplates) had to be changed. A deadline of 23 November was set. The consequences for those who failed to comply would be severe. For Kuwaitis this meant giving up their nationality and admitting that there was no such country as Kuwait, that it was now the 19th province and, by implication, had never existed except in the minds of the imperialists who had created it. This in any case was quite untrue, for Kuwait had never been created by imperialists, but from its inception in the mid-eighteenth century was an independent country ruled by a sheikhly family. Before that, Kuwait had probably been a series of small fishing villages with tribal allegiances. Those villages accepted the rule of the forebears of the present Al Sabah family, and Kuwait gradually became an important trading and pearl-fishing country. Its citizens travelled as far afield as Syria and by sea to East Africa and India. By contrast, Iraq and Jordan were imperial creations. Both had been carved into kingdoms by the British following the collapse of the Ottoman Empire in the early twentieth century. Kuwait had never fallen under the direct jurisdiction of the Ottomans, or for that matter the British.

Everyone was ordered to go to the passport building in the district of Farwaniya to begin the paperwork to change their nationality. To the best of my knowledge hardly any Kuwaitis went along. Some, unable to bear the psychological trauma, left the country. Failure to change nationality debarred one from being able to drive, obtain petrol, or receive hospital treatment from the now much-depleted government hospitals. It also meant being unable to obtain the now essential ration cards for basic foods such as milk, sugar, rice, flour and cooking oil. To add to the blow, the Kuwaiti dinar was now to be replaced by the worthless Iraqi dinar. The Iraqis had been keen collectors of Kuwaiti dinars and had devised all kinds of schemes for parting them from their owners. Now the soldiers at road checks were ordered to tear them up and throw them to the wind. But if they could, they would slip them into their pockets or tuck them behind their belts. Those who were able to tried to estimate how many Kuwaiti dinars they would have to change into Iraqi dinars and then pray that the situation would change and Kuwait would be freed.

Nationals of countries supporting the Coalition were told to report to one of the sports clubs to exchange their Kuwaiti residence permits for Iraqi ones. After being humiliated by officials who swore at them and threw their passports around, most of these people ended up having to pay large bribes to get their documentation in order. Some were arrested for failing to do anything about changing their papers.

The Kuwaitis gritted their teeth and, despite the strain of never knowing what would happen next, determined to change nothing and to do nothing. Though non-Kuwaitis had little choice but to change their numberplates (and many used their cars to help Kuwaitis go out and find food), cars with their original numberplates continued to be seen on the roads. Fortunately the Iraqis were inefficient and, given that the computers had been either smashed or stolen, all changes had to be made by hand. When people were stopped at roadblocks and challenged for still having their original numberplates, they would maintain that the queues were enormous and that they could not help it if their papers had not yet been issued.

One Kuwaiti woman who knew that ration cards were being issued, but had obviously misunderstood the regulations, waited her turn in line to fill in the papers. She asked the man at the grille for ration card papers and he said, 'Where's your ID?' Opening her bag, she took it out and showed it to him.

'You're not entitled to them,' he said glaring at her.

'You have to go and get your ID changed to the Iraqi 19th province first. Go and do that and you can have ration cards; if you won't then you can starve.'

The woman slammed her hand down on the ledge, snatched up her Kuwaiti ID card and shouted, 'I would rather starve first. You can grind me into the dust, but I will *never* be anything but a Kuwaiti.'

Though everyone agreed with this bravely expressed sentiment, I have to admit that occasionally my imagination took over and I privately wondered what it would feel like to die slowly of starvation. However, one derived some comfort from the thought that at least we would all be suffering together. But no one intended to give way. There were deadlines for the car numberplates and deadlines for the IDs and when the first one arrived we all wondered whether there would be shootings, or hangings, or what. As an adult, particularly an older adult, one felt that it did not matter that much, but for the young and the very young it would be terrible in all respects. The young were in as much danger of ill treatment from the Iraqis as the adults; there are records of children of under 10 years of age and men and women of over 80 being tortured and imprisoned.

In the post that arrived one day via a friend who had come from Jordan was a letter plus the name and telephone number of the person to whom it should be delivered. It came from a Zambian doctor who had been on a course in England in July. His Kuwaiti wife and three small children had been living in the family house and he had been due to arrive back shortly after the invasion. Since that time he had heard nothing whatsoever about his family and had no idea what had happened to them. He had managed to contact my husband in England who arranged to get a letter through to Kuwait.

I dialled the number and in a low tone in English enquired if Sitt Ayesha were there. The answer came back quickly, 'No, she was not in Kuwait, she was out of the country and had left long ago.' Knowing that this was unlikely, I persisted, saying I had news of her husband and that I might ring back later. Later I dialled once and this time a young boy answered. There was a pause when I asked after Ayesha, the phone was handed over and cautiously a voice said, 'Yes?' Rapidly I said there was a letter which I would try to deliver soon. Then politely dropping the subject we asked each other how things were and put the phones down.

A day or so later, using a car with a changed numberplate and carrying our unchanged IDs and the precious letter, we set off. On the way we drove past the teachers' flats. The area was dirty. There were piles of rubbish bags lying around and overfilled skips with their complement of scrawny big-eyed cats. We turned in near the flats, slowing down slightly so as to see as much as we could as we went past. The teachers park their cars in the compound when they go on holiday and we could tell that many had been damaged and that the most popular ones had already been stolen. All our guards had left and although the main door to the flats had been locked and chained as securely as possible, the doors had been broken open and some of the flats had already been looted. In many areas the going rate for a flat with its contents had been between 200 and 300 Kuwaiti dinars. When our financial manager Mr John and his assistant Mr Mathew, who lived elsewhere, eventually returned to Kuwait they found literally nothing in their flats: even the light switches and hot water boilers had been removed. One of their friends had gone over to see if she could rescue anything, but it was very dangerous for legitimate people to be caught and by the time she arrived, the flats had been cleared. That particular section had been looted, not by Iraqis, but by pro-Iraqi Arab nationals, who openly removed the contents of many people's flats. Teenagers and even their parents were wandering through the blocks turning over what was left. In fact these particular nationals made several offers to buy the teachers' flats. Their answer to my refusal was, 'Well, you might just as well have sold them, as everything will be taken anyway.' In retrospect there is something to be said for completely emptied flats. There can be no arguments later on and everyone has to begin again, which can solve a number of problems!

We then decided to see if we could buy some eggs from the Amman Street market. Most of Kuwait's regular shops had been looted and were now totally desolate, with their windows broken and the remains of their contents lying at crazy angles on the ground. The owner of a material shop told me later that his high-quality fabrics had totally disappeared, with the rest just trashed and the fitments broken. Some shop owners had managed to find steel frames to weld across their shop fronts, but even then, patient and persistent attempts had been made to peel back the steel like sardine tins. Occasionally a thief had had some success. Now, instead of shops, exceedingly dirty and smelly street markets had sprung up and were operating either on the ground or from orange boxes amongst overflowing and semi-burning rubbish skips. One of the biggest and dirtiest of these was down a main street called Sha'ara Amman. Food (and the money with which to buy it) became an obsession, especially for people with children. At the beginning, just after the invasion, all sorts of electronic equipment was being sold on the streets, but as time went on all that remained were bottles of shampoo, sometimes lentils, bars of melted and remelted chocolate and other items for which, under the circumstances, people had little use.

Until the air war Jordan seemed to have broken sanctions with impunity and supplies of eggs, tomatoes and onions were to be had — at a price. Jordanian tomatoes were smooth, round and beautiful, and a small box cost KD 27 (approximately £54 sterling), while the disfigured, pitted and black-spotted Iraqi ones were half that price. As one might imagine, life was practically impossible for people with children and little money, but anyone who received anything shared it out with their less fortunate neighbours and, for as long as they could, women packed their cars with supplies and delivered them to those in desperate need.

There are strong grounds for suspecting that Jordan broke more than food sanctions. After the liberation everyone in Kuwait was struck by the number of crates and boxes of ammunition lying absolutely everywhere with 'GHQ Royal Jordanian Army' printed clearly on them. One Jordanian lorry driver told my husband that he had been well paid to drive 'supplies' into Iraq along the main highway. As he approached the border, he would leave the main road and travel along desert paths to where Iraqi soldiers would be waiting to guide him into Iraq. This had continued until the Allies began to bomb the lorries heavily, calling down on their heads the wrath of the peace activists, who made great and indignant noises about 'innocent' drivers being killed. We certainly knew that lorries carrying vegetables and driven mainly by Jordanians were arriving in Kuwait and, judging from the quantity of arms that were left behind, it seems possible that other items might have come in as well.

In the Sha'ara Amman there were piles of boxed eggs from Jordan, brown ones and white ones, selling at about KD 9 (about £18 sterling) for 24, which meant that every single egg had been inspected closely to see that there were no bad ones. Cheap machine-embroidered house dresses, almost certainly stolen from some shop or store, started at KD 75, but it would be surprising if any of these were sold. The air here, as in fact in most districts, smelled as if slightly rotten kebabs were being burned in the rubbish dumps. Though the dumps were set alight every day, with the wind blowing up and distributing the foetid ash, the area they covered seemed to be spreading in a slow-moving slightly wave-like manner. Apart from the cats, people would also inspect the dumps, for one person's rubbish could be another one's treasure. Certainly they would scuffle about to see if there was anything to feed to the chickens that many had taken to keeping. We stared at the grey, drawn faces around us, bought a carton of brown eggs and decided we had better get on and try to deliver the letter to the doctor's wife.

We drove along side roads, keeping a watch out for roadblocks so as to avoid them as far as possible. The prospect of chemical warfare had once again raised its ugly head and Iraqi television was constantly showing programmes about what to do in the event of an 'attack'. It grandly announced that every person in Iraq would be issued with a gas mask, though no mention was made of the '19th province'. The Kuwaiti Resistance had already set up first-aid classes and distributed notices about what to do in the event of chemical warfare, bombing and suchlike. But of course there were no gas masks, nor any means of obtaining them. The best anyone could hope to do was to make a face mask by wrapping a piece of cloth around some charcoal.

Ahead of us was an unavoidable roadblock and we joined the queue of slow moving cars. To our amazement, the soldiers were wearing gas masks and looking rather pleased with themselves. Presumably this was a rather unsubtle way of pointing out to the population that the army was protected and that we were not. I do not know if this was a widespread action, as I only saw it happen in three places in that particular district (in which there were many Kuwaitis). Truth to tell, in our car at least, we found a certain grim humour in the situation and everyone began to giggle slightly hysterically and to tell 'black jokes'.

As we drew alongside to present our IDs we composed ourselves to present an almost polite, expressionless face. Our friend driving the car was an Iraqi of long residence in Kuwait whose family in Basra had suffered considerably under the Saddam regime. Ten years before, his mother-in-law, a *Basrawiya* (from Basra) with Persian forebears, had been woken one night by a visit from the *Mukhabarat*. She was taken from her house and, apparently, pushed over the border into

Iran. She was an elderly woman who had never in fact been out of Basra in her life. Though careful enquiries were made over a long period, she was never heard of again. Many others like her suffered the same fate.

The soldiers spoke echoingly from behind their gas masks and seemed to delight in what they were wearing. They glanced at the driver's ID, peered into the back seat of the car and waved us on, and the car continued uninterrupted until we reached Faiha. Although we had all torn down road signs and removed house numbers at the beginning of the invasion, it had never crossed my mind that it would be quite so difficult to find someone's house. Every district is divided into smaller quarters and then again, rather haphazardly, into street and house numbers. At the best of times it is difficult to find one's way around Kuwait, though it had been improving. As we moved along the road we realized that absolutely everything had been taken away. There were no house numbers on any of the doors, nor in fact anything to indicate who lived there. It was not a district that any of us knew very well. Because everyone tended to remain indoors, there were few people on the road. The traffic was minimal and, at least as far as we could tell, there were no *Mukhabarat* patrolling the streets in their dark glasses and newly acquired cars. We could now tell we were going to have a hard time trying to deliver the letter. Although the roads were fortunately fairly empty of traffic, it looked suspicious to keep wandering slowly around and around.

By a stroke of luck, half hidden at the corner of a street by overgrown and broken plants, I saw what appeared to be the remains of a street number. Assuming that it was where it had originally been thrown the road we required had to be somewhere nearby. Covering it up carefully again, we saw a man turning the corner at the end of the street. I chased after him and somewhat naively asked if he knew where the house we were looking for was. Blandly he replied that he did not live in this area at all and therefore did not know who lived in the surrounding houses. I realized that something really bad must have happened in this particular place. In our brief telephone conversations about the letter little was said about her location and it would have been risky to have enlarged on the subject.

We then began to try and work out logically from what little we knew which street it could be, for we did at least seem to have arrived in roughly the correct place. As we were slowly cruising around looking for possible 'clues', I saw a middle-aged woman come out of a house and walk towards a parked car. Other women were gathered in the doorway to see her off. I decided to have one more try to see if she knew how to find the house.

She looked at me slightly suspiciously and remarked. 'You're English aren't you? Why haven't you gone?'

'I'm married to a Kuwaiti, and I've been here too long to go. I don't want to leave; are you staying?' I asked.

'It's my country. I'm not leaving either,' she replied.

We both cursed the invaders and the occupation, which on reflection could have been a dangerous thing to do, for listening ears were everywhere and for all either of us knew we might have been overheard. By now we had been trying to find the house for well over two hours and, having explained hesitantly that we were delivering a letter, I asked if we could use the telephone in the house she had just left. Rather nervously the women showed us to a table on which there was a phone and I rang the number and said we were near a mosque. It was better not to ask for a description of where she lived. We agreed to meet by the mosque.

We guessed that we had been quite close to her house, but there was absolutely no indication that we would have been able to find it. She came out quickly, followed by her children, to where we were standing, a bit worried that we looked suspicious. We found out why the residents had been particularly careful to whom they talked. It is a district in which many Kuwaitis live and they had put up a considerable resistance at the beginning of August. On a number of occasions the army had surrounded the entire quarter and moved through every house arresting all men over the age of 15. They had been thrown into trucks and buses, beaten and then taken away. The children had also been threatened and the residents were always on the watch out for the army's return, much in the way that we spent most of our time looking out of our windows. One did not have to do too much to get oneself shot. One young man, who was not active in the Resistance, had been standing on his doorstep just outside his house and was about to go inside, when a couple of jeeps full of armed soldiers passed by. They shouted at him roughly to get back inside. When he replied that he was standing on his own doorstep, he was casually shot dead there and then. Not long afterwards, his brother, who was active in the Resistance, was caught, brought to the same doorstep, shot dead and left there as a lesson to the neighbours. This practice of bringing prisoners to their own houses to be shot dead, often in the presence of their families, was very common.

The days passed in a mixture of apprehensive boredom and terrifying excitement, interspersed with moments of watching or listening to what was happening on the political scene. We watched the procession of world leaders, ex-prime ministers and politicians arriving in Iraq to talk to Saddam Hussein. He obviously basked in all the attention being paid to him, until it became too time-consuming to cope with any longer and the hostages were all released. Everyone saw the programme in which the Iraqi president scoffed at the high-tech armaments being lined up against Iraq and, to thunderous clapping from his audience, mentioned how 'one of our shepherds had seen the Stealth plane passing overhead', which would in fact have been quite impossible for anyone to have seen. We listened to political analysts talking endlessly and wondered how many of them were merely armchair theoreticians. We listened to Gulf Link from Britain, which had been set up for the benefit of the hostages and people in hiding. If we recognized any names and knew how they could be contacted, we would phone through messages in our best cryptic language. Once someone sent Barbara Bodine at the American Embassy her grateful thanks for all that had been done to help her leave Kuwait. At another time a group of men with a misplaced sense of humour told their hostage friend that they 'had been playing all the games he liked, drinking a glass or two of beer and saluting him, their thoughts were with him, although his gran thought the whole thing was a soap opera serial'. The Arabic services of the BBC, Monte Carlo and Voice of America became most unpopular in Kuwait because of their perceived bias in favour of Iraq. Many, and that included my husband, eventually refused to listen, or tuned in only occasionally and then always finding the news biased in favour of Iraq. Sometimes I too felt that the English-language side of the BBC was not quite living up to its reputation for impartiality.

Every three weeks or so the Iraqi regiment in the school was changed and a new round of looting, both within the school and in the district at large, would take place. The so-called elite Republican

Guards had now taken over the Iranian school, which was directly down the road from our house. They set up a big artillery gun on top of the roof, which swivelled slowly round and round all day. We all named the gunner, or more accurately the series of gunners, 'Kathem'. Those who sat atop the nine spectacular black and white striped mushroom-like water towers across the ring road further away, were known as 'Nathem'. Kathem and Nathem are the Iraqi equivalents of the English 'John Smith'. Unlike soldiers of the People's Army, as Republican Guards Kathem and Nathem were professionals and took some care of their equipment. They would clean it carefully and, after ferocious bursts of shooting, would oil the parts or do whatever was necessary to keep their guns operational. As far as we could see, the only other exercise the army took (professional or otherwise) was looting, or arresting and beating up people.

By the time the army had been occupying our school for about a month, the soldiers had got to know Abu Ali, Abu Yaseen, Nadr and a couple of the guards by name. Abu Ali tried to continue watering the trees, which the army had no intention of doing. Abu Yaseen had already been beaten up a number of times for his sharp remarks, while Nadr was thought to be an electrician. On one occasion he was picked up, taken into school and told to set up a television aerial for the soldiers and to get the main air-conditioning machines to work. He had no intention of touching the air-conditioning, but was quite keen to do the aerial in the hope that the men would be able to watch programmes from Dubai and Sharjah and not just from Baghdad. As he came into what had been the administration office, he saw the commander, pistol strapped round his waist, sitting on the now dirty seats with the table in front of him plastered with dirty cups, unwashed pots, cigarette ends and sticky tea marks, with a few ants scuttling frenziedly around.

Nadr glanced about at the pro-Saddam graffiti all over the walls and painted in huge letters on the road. He took in the half-opened broken drawers and the strewn papers fluttering through the doorway in the hot breeze. This particular group belonged to the *Jesh Sha'abi* (or People's Army) and the main gates were guarded by what can only be described as 'knackered' old men holding rifles. The more alert younger ones were possibly informers and in the intelligence division. The People's Army was made up of non-professional volunteers who were given a few days' military training and then sent off for duty. During the Iraq–Iran war they had sometimes been used as 'cannon fodder', leaving the professionals to follow behind for the kill. They ranged from boys barely into their early teens to octogenarians. One of the groups at the school contained a grandfather and his grandson.

As he was walking towards the commander, Nadr's heart sank at the sight of the disorder and damage, which obviously extended throughout the school. He greeted the officer politely but then, upset at what he was seeing, unthinkingly snapped, 'You're the commander. Why is the place so filthy? Isn't there anyone who would at least wipe the table? Don't you tell the soldiers what to do?' The man looked at him, vaguely cleared a space on the table and mumbled, 'Go and look at the aerial and then do something about the air-conditioning.' They all went down the steps into the yard, an informer included, and stood discussing the TV aerial. One man said hopefully, 'It would be nice if the TV worked, I'd like to see other pro—.' He glanced at the informer and said firmly, 'Baghdad, it would be so nice to be able to watch Baghdad again.'

Nadr had no intention of making the Iraqi Army comfortable by working on the central air-conditioning machinery. The box air-conditioners that had been in the school had already been removed and, presumably, sold. He passed the prayer room, with its door hanging ajar, and caught a glimpse of the disorder inside, the army boots scattered around the floor, dust lying thickly everywhere. There was a smell wafting out as if some bad meat had been left lying around. As he and the soldier climbed the stairs towards the antenna on the top of the roof, the informer was left behind for a short while. The soldier was a middle-aged man with nine children, who said he had worked in a store in Baghdad before joining the People's Army.

He and his family lived with his parents in a two-roomed house. Nadr asked if under these circumstances he was happy to have so many children to try and support. The man said 'No', not in those conditions. So did they not know about methods of birth control in Iraq? 'Of course,' was the slightly irritated reply, but pills of any kind were quite beyond their purse. He was well aware that there were birth control operations but these were beyond his reach as well. The tragedy is that Iraq is one of the richest nations, yet massive amounts of money had been spent, not on education, health and raising the standard of living, but on armaments. It did not help either that the developed world had been so keen to sell more and more war technology to Iraq.

When Nadr had set up the antenna and told them he was unable to deal with the central air-conditioning because certain key elements had been removed, he left. He, Abu Ali and Abu Yaseen then kept out of sight as much as possible until the group were moved on and another arrived who knew nothing about them. Our particular area now seemed to be full of soldiers of every kind, not only at the bottom of the road in the Iranian school and surrounding the French and Chinese embassies, but also over and under all the motorway bridges. They were billeted in the nearby government schools as well as in the police station from which the women demonstrators had been shot. We were perpetually expecting and watching out for more house searches, especially since soldiers were so frequently being found dead near their posts in the early morning.

Bill, who phoned from time to time, rang me up after a particularly horrendous experience in his flat. One night four armed Iraqis and Palestinians had forced an entry into the theoretically empty block of flats in which he was living. Bill and the other man had been tied up while, with guns held to their heads, the gunmen had proceeded to empty the flats of their contents. It was a nightmarish situation and one in which they could have easily been shot dead or turned over to the army as hostages. In between being tied up, having guns held to their heads and being threatened with death, Bill (his flat mate was busy making tea for them all) was invited by one of the Iraqi gunmen to lunch 'one day' at his house in Baghdad. The gunmen were anxious to leave before the night-time curfew ended, and went away having removed nearly everything, including food, but leaving one telephone. This was the lifeline through which the Resistance was able to move Bill to yet another hideout, where he managed to survive uncaught until all the hostages and men in hiding were allowed to leave in early December.

Early each morning, having carefully looking outside through every window, I would go downstairs and out onto the silent road to stare cautiously up at Kathem seated on his artillery gun. I was convinced that if he and his gun were gone, it would mean that the Iraqis were leaving Kuwait. Each morning, to my disappointment, he was still there. As the months went by and it became colder, he became more huddled up in his seat, or would lean against the wall rubbing his hands together and trying to catch the sun. But he and his gun were always there. I would then unlock the side gates to my son's house (the main ones had blocks of wood battened across them) and slide through the space left between them and the cars to see if everything outside were intact. After glancing up at the front of the house on one occasion, I moved towards the front door and, to my horror, saw a whole window lying on the ground, with bits and pieces of broken wood scattered around. The house had been broken into and there was no sign or sound of Keaton. Many thoughts went through my head as I stared through the empty window into the sitting room. One of the red cushions had the clear imprint of an army boot on it, all the side tables had been thrown about and some of the glass jars and their shelves had been broken. Had Keaton been killed, or perhaps injured, or arrested, or—?

In a sense I was relieved that Nita (the Filipina maid) had left as a refugee a few days earlier. I could not bear to think of what might have happened to her had she been there and been caught by the soldiers. I ran back to fetch Nadr (whom I had to wake up) and when we returned we climbed through the window and into the house. It had been fairly thoroughly ransacked. All the contents of the cupboards had been thrown about and there was no sign of Keaton at all. We walked around calling him in a low voice and were preparing to find a ladder to get ourselves into the air-conditioning ducts where we hoped he had taken refuge when, to our immense relief, he crawled out of the ducts, where he had once again been hiding for at least six hours.

He had fortunately been sleeping on the raised loft close to a duct opening when he had once again woken up to hear the rattle of rifles, loud voices and heavy army boots tramping through the house. He froze on his mattress as the door was pushed open and men trooped in and proceeded to throw open the cupboards and pull out the drawers. After a while they moved away to another part of the house and he took advantage of the respite to pull himself and the mattress through the opening and down into the ducts. Hardly had he done that when the men were back again, laughing and talking. This time they climbed up onto the ledge, opened the hatch and shone a torch down. Keaton kept as still as possible and the duct was long, so seeing

111

nothing the men moved on to more interesting pursuits. They spent most of the night going up and down stairs, picking and choosing what they fancied and, worse, taking most of the food in the freezer and refrigerator. Oddly enough they did not apparently go down to the basement, perhaps because the lights had fused there and they disliked the dark heavy feeling it gave of being nearly underground. The door to the museum library was in any case concealed by broken boxes and large pieces of cardboard.

Keaton was not sure when they finally left, but had barely dared breathe at one point when they had stood near to a grille within a few feet of his head. The soldiers had stolen most of the electrical goods in the house, many of my son's suits and all of Keaton's clothing. We were fortunate in that, although they left such a mess behind, they did not, as quite often happened, set fire to anything, or spray-paint or urinate around the place. Shortly after Keaton's experience, our director's house was broken into again and things were removed, but this time not by Iraqis. The neighbours had seen armed men (not soldiers) entering all the empty houses and loading things onto a trailer they had brought with them. We had already removed everything we could of any value from the house and had left the tables and chairs askew in the hopes that other thieves would be discouraged. I noticed with some surprise that all Mr Rodgers's suits had been left hanging neatly on the cupboard rail. Mr Rodgers noticed the same thing when he eventually returned to the house, and it was only when he was getting dressed for a formal occasion that he discovered that the jackets were all there but that every single pair of trousers had been stolen.

After that experience Keaton continued to sleep by the air-conditioning ducts. Nadr and Abu Ali checked all the windows, replaced the broken one and put car grease along the top of the garden fence. Nadr decided to set up an electronic system that would alert us if anyone broke into the house. All of this kept us busy but it in no way deterred the Republicans from down the road from going on the prowl from about midnight until dawn.

For the next 10 or so nights we and our neighbours seemed to be objects of considerable interest to the soldiers who set out to plunder both empty and occupied houses. Nadr kept watch from the roof and, on the night after Keaton's break-in, saw an army pick-up loaded with soldiers drive up the road. The van dropped the men off, three at a

During the air war the Tornados and B52s dropped their bombs then circled the sky.
At first the Iraqis shot at them unavailingly out of frustration.

Right. The old part of the Seif Palace.

Below. Even the old wooden trading boats (dhows) had been burned and sunk.

Above. Photograph secretly taken at one of the women's demonstrations that took place over many districts in Kuwait. *Below.* Liberation! 26 February 1991.

Another of the 732 oil fires; in the forground one of the massive oil lakes left all over the desert

Above. Sometimes the clouds of smoke blew out to sea or elsewhere, but mostly they hung over Kuwait.
Below. It was frightening driving in the oil fields as often it was nearly impossible to see anything (photo: Kuwait Oil Company).

Right. Nadr working on mending air condition-ers, water tanks and other machinery. Due to lack of maintenance and spare parts they were always breaking down.

Below. In spite of everything the school was ready to open 14 September 1991.

ght. Removing the
'ecoy' from the
pboards. The
rpenters had hastily
ade them to conceal
the storage
pboards.

Left. Mr Rajab
unblocking the
connection between
the two sides of the
museum.

Strings of bullets lay everywhere, in streets, houses, on the roads and in the desert

time, at different points (their rifles were left behind on the bottom of the truck) and sneakily they crept towards the various houses. Then, with his voice echoing loudly, Nadr roared, *'Harami, harami!'* (thieves, thieves).

With my window open as usual, I woke with a start, leapt out of bed and, looking outside, saw what Nadr had not seen. Creeping around our yard as quietly as their army boots would allow, their fingers poking into this and that and obviously about to break and enter were the Red Berets from down the road. I ran to the other side of the house to take a look next door. There they were down in the sunken court-yard, removing things from the various cartons our neighbour had placed there out of sight for safety. Each man had a little pile of goodies he intended to take when he left. One had found a T-shirt, which he was holding up against himself for size, turning and twisting about trying to imagine how he would look in it.

Hearing Nadr shouting the men all began to run away and out of sight as fast as they could. In theory stealing from private homes was illegal. News of the massive looting and theft from Kuwait had reached the outside world and now we all had a right to complain.

We had noticed that most of them were not carrying arms, having left them behind in the bottom of the truck. Indignantly (and in retro-spect unwisely) we grabbed broomsticks and rushed outside, waving them about wildly and hoping to appear ferocious. We stood around watching the other houses, many of whose residents had been woken up by Nadr's shouting and were standing outside their doors looking indignantly around. The sound of a humming engine was the first sign that something was coming back over the sand. Up the pavement and onto the sand lurched a wanette with three Red Berets standing up in the back. We swelled out our chests and waved our sticks menacingly. To our amazement, as their heads turned in our direction, they yelled desperately over the drone of the engine, 'To the right, to the right, go to the right.' The driver glanced in our direction and moved off to the right away from us.

Because they had seemed so interested in the cartons in the court-yard, Nadr hastily set up a howler system on its steps. We had a feeling that they might return when the night quietened down again. While he was doing that I decided to let the Saluki stay next door as a further alarm, for he tended to like barking. Being desert hunting dogs

Salukis have an amazing turn of speed and it is pure poetry to watch one running in the sand — not unlike a cheetah in this respect. They are similar to but more beautiful than lurchers. In the old days they used to live with the Bedouin as part of the family and shared the hard life with them, helping to fill the cooking pot. Although they bark a good deal they are not guard dogs and I should have known better than to have put him in the other house. He did not mind running outside on the sand or in the now empty road, but to go over and sleep next door was not his idea of fun. He whined pitifully when I tried to get him to follow me and then collapsed in a little heap on the ground when I attempted to push him. I firmly picked him up, his long slender legs waving about in protest and put him down in the courtyard where he lay shivering in dismay. Then he hid behind a pillar. When I opened the gate slightly the next morning, with a Saluki smile on his face he ran joyfully out and back to *his* garden.

For the next few nights we had hardly any sleep as the soldiers roamed from one place and one side of the block to another. Keaton slept in the ducts and we snatched snoozes with one ear open all the time. As Nadr was looking out of the window towards the sunken courtyard early one morning, he saw a soldier creeping over the fence, his fingers slipping and sliding on the grease. The soldier managed to heave himself up and was obviously coming back for the pile of clothing that he had left before on the previous occasion. Nadr watched him tiptoe towards (and get halfway down) the steps and then pressed the button on the howler, which screamed into the silence like the siren of a police car. The man leapt into the air, turned up the stairs and paused to gaze longingly at 'his bundle' below before fear took over and he raced up and over the fence, slipping slightly on the grease, and down the road to his barracks.

All these attempts at breaking into and entering even occupied houses eventually became so bad that, along with some other men, Nadr went to complain at the police station. The officials there looked sour and disinterested and merely said they would investigate and to 'come back in two and a half days' time', which in effect meant that nothing was going to be done. Nadr decided instead to go down to the Iranian school and to speak to their commander, for in our area at least the Red Berets from there seemed to be the main culprits. The particular officer to whom Nadr spoke was quite a young man, who had fought in the Iraq–Iran war and had a good deal of army experience. He denied that any such thing as looting was taking place; his men did not do things, but anyway he would make sure that they were controlled. The situation was greatly improved by the presentation of a nice watch and a pen and pencil pack. The looting never did stop and we always had to remain on the alert, but we did at least manage to get some sleep and things were never quite as bad again as they had been during those 10 days.

We had hardly recovered from the spate of attempted robberies when Nadr was rung up by an Egyptian guard, who had remained at his post in a block of flats opposite that of the teachers. He had done his best to keep an eye on all the surrounding property and, while unable to prevent breaking and entering, he would at least ring to say if the main door bolts had once again been cut or another car had disappeared. One day an Iraqi policeman from the Jabriya police station, who had been removing teachers' cars, walked up to the guard, pointed out some and said, 'Make sure that no-one touches these as every day I am going to take one.' That was when the guard rang up to report the probable theft of more cars.

All that could be done was to try and immobilize those that were left and make them as difficult as possible to remove. Grabbing their tools, Nadr and Abu Ali went straight off to the flats to remove wheels and to hide distributor heads, contacts and batteries. They decided to put everything down in a basement under the flats. With the more easily accessible flats receiving the most attention, this part of the building was only broken into towards the end of the occupation, because its door was inconspicuously placed.

Watched by the guard and keeping a cautious eye on the road, Nadr and Abu Ali began to disconnect and remove batteries. Now and again a car passed by. The Iraqis had given up trying to make the Kuwaitis change their car numberplates and now it had become possible to change plates without losing one's nationality. The laws about rationing and health facilities were not, however, altered and no Kuwaitis could obtain rations or health care without their new nationality papers. Because people so hated and resented the new numbers, they would change the number on an old car and then use it only for shopping and buying petrol, which they would then siphon off into cars that had not been changed. In that way there could be as few changes as possible.

It was still illegal for a car with an old numberplate to be filled up at a petrol station, but the Kurdish soldiers sometimes allowed them to get away with it, though this was all a matter of luck. When one Kuwaiti's car was waved in by the Kurdish guards and the Palestinian at the pump refused to fill it because the number was illegal, the Kuwaiti stepped out of his car, stared fixedly at the petrol pump attendant for a couple of seconds and said, 'I will not forget your face. I advise you not to be here when Kuwait is liberated.'

As Nadr and Abu Ali squatted on the ground, slowly removing wheels and contacts, their minds were half on the road in case roving army personnel became interested in what they were doing. They became aware that a large Mercedes had driven round the block and had now returned. It drew to a stop and out stepped an Iraqi policeman, his hand on the gun at his waist and a frown on his face. As he strode towards them he shouted, 'Come, come, what are you doing, stealing other people's cars, eh?' Nadr stood up and replied, 'We're not stealing. These flats belong to my school and we are looking after the cars.'

Upon which the man asked to see both the car books and Nadr's identity card, so that they could check that they matched. The car books were naturally in the possession of their owners and would obviously not have matched Nadr's papers. Whereupon the policeman arrested Nadr, Abu Ali and even the guard who had been watching them work. They were all marched off at gunpoint, forced into the Mercedes and driven away to the Jabriya police station. They realized from the policeman's expression that he must have been the person who had been removing the cars and that he viewed them as *his* property. They also realized that they were now in extreme danger because no one would know they had been arrested until it was too late. None of them was under any illusions about their likely fate.

On their arrival at the police station, which was not very far from the flats, they were shoved roughly into a room. Nadr and Abu Ali began to explain once more that the cars belonged to teachers from the school, that quite a number had already disappeared and that they were, as school officials, trying to prevent the rest from being taken. None of this impressed the police authorities, least of all the man who had been slowly removing the cars and no doubt selling them or trans-porting them back to Iraq. He glowered at them and told them they were liars and thieves. Once a file had been opened on them, people accused of theft would be transported to Basra for trial. According to some people we knew, each accused person was assigned a lawyer, but this did not seem to have much effect on the outcome of the trial. If one were lucky, one might get away with a prison term, but thieves were more likely to be sentenced to hang.

One European, who had not at that point been a potential hostage, had attempted to drive across the border into Iran. However, he was arrested, taken to the prison in Basra and put into a cell with a number of other people. They were all badly fed and the cells were overcrowded and dirty, but the most traumatic aspect of his experience was hearing the screams of people being tortured further down the corridor. And I believe he occasionally caught a brief glimpse of some of them. After about six weeks and still not knowing why he had been arrested, he was given a trial he could not follow and a lawyer he barely understood. However, he was acquitted and released from gaol. He was then driving towards Baghdad to complete his exit papers when he was arrested once more, again for no apparent reason, and found himself back in prison. He was eventually reacquitted and this time managed to return to his country.

Nadr, Abu Ali and the guard had a couple of strokes of good luck. For some reason the man in charge of opening files on prisoners was not there and, incensed at what he saw as *his* cars being incapacitated, the policeman's partner in theft had gone off to the flats in a rage to lecture another guard in the vicinity. This man was in fact an employee who had worked on the school's new teacher flats in another district and had been watching from a distance when the three men were arrested. As soon as he realized where they had been taken he phoned Abu Ali's wife and she told me.

While we sat in a panic wondering how we could prove their innocence and trying to remember the names of parents who had been officials at the Iraqi Embassy, Nadr, Abu Ali and the guard remained in the station. While they were sitting there arguing with the man who had arrested them, another man strode in. He looked around, walked up to Nadr and, poking his finger at Nadr's chest and shaking his head sternly, said 'Aren't you ashamed of being a thief, stealing other people's cars?'

Bug-eyed and unable to reply Nadr could only stare at him, for emblazoned across the man's T-shirted chest was written NEW ENGLISH SCHOOL; he was wearing one of the shirts stolen from the school storeroom, in fact from the same batch later seen for sale on a Baghdad pavement.

Nadr, Abu Ali and the guard sat in the police station for six more tension-filled and nerve-racking hours. Sometimes they argued with the officer, who was anxiously waiting for the file clerk to return. The sooner they could be officially charged and their files prepared the better it would be for him. At one point the officer stood up and, before leaving the room, loudly snapped at the soldier on guard, 'If they move, shoot them.' As time passed the chances of the file clerk coming back on duty became greater and greater. Abu Ali's wife was trying desperately to find people who might be able to help. I was scouring my telephone numbers and looking through whatever we had managed to rescue from the school by way of official papers — and all the while we were conscious that we might not be able to save them.

In the end, by a most fortunate combination of the clerk not returning, me finding a few documents and Abu Ali's wife managing to contact an Iraqi Embassy parent (who was most likely in the *Mukhabarat*), all three men were released. As they left the station they were told 'not to do such things again'. The parent commented that had the files been made out, even he would have been unable to do very much.

After that experience none of us even considered going past the flats for quite some time. The guard still let us know when chains were broken. The remaining cars stayed there (though with bits of their engines disappearing, wheels gone and windows gradually being broken) and a pall of dust settled over the remains.

Shortly after Nadr and Abu Ali's arrest, we heard that a number of empty flats in Kuwait were to be taken over by families from Iraq. Soon after the invasion many of these *makhakirah* (settlers) had arrived in Kuwait and it is possible that some of the new arrivals in outlying districts were Iraqi. Just over halfway through the occupation other people, some of whom were quite probably from Iraq, moved into a few flats and villas not far from us. Around the time of the air war we were told that all newcomers had been ordered to return to Iraq and indeed some of the people in those flats moved out and were not seen again. Ultimately all orders came from Saddam Hussein personally. We could see from the television that he did not brook much opposition or disagreement. On viewing a meeting of the Iraqi Parliament we were shocked at the close attention paid to what he said, at the way even dignified men much older than him appeared to 'drink in' his words of wisdom. One particularly interesting programme showed the *Raees* (Saddam) visiting a bunker somewhere in the Kuwaiti desert to study the war situation with his top military men. At that particular moment, for it was just before the air war and things cannot have looked good to professional soldiers (there were problems with petrol supplies, as well as with securing water and food for the army), we detected a grimness, almost a coldness, in the faces of his commanders and a lack of direct eye contact. The young Red Beret military note-taker accompanying the party stood out amongst all the bleak-faced men, for he was incredibly cheerful, good-looking and literally shining with health.

Jokes of all kinds, but mostly black humour ones, abounded throughout the occupation. One of the more popular ones concerned a visit by Saddam to a village in the north of Iraq. On one of his walkabouts in his 'man of the people' guise (which would feature a couple of times each day on television) he walked up to a group of villagers, paused in front of a man whose small son was gazing up at the president, jovially bent down and, patting the boy on the head, asked, 'Do you know who I am?' The boy looked at him with interest, turned to his father and said,' Is he the one you spit at every day?' In a panic the father said loudly, 'Who is this boy, who's son is he?'

Another joke that did the rounds during the air war (which may even have contained a grain of truth) concerned Iraqi soldiers billeted in one of the government schools. At that time everybody was expecting a seaborne landing, possibly with marines being parachuted in as well. The school lay on the edge of a large square surrounded by private houses and nearby there was an electricity substation. In the middle of a morning in which there had been some shooting something in the substation exploded with a terrific force. The rumour went round the barracks that the Americans had landed and many of the soldiers

119

rushed out into the road clutching their guns. They ran up to the occupied houses and hammered on their doors until they were opened. 'If we give you our guns, will you give us a *dishdasha*?' they asked. *Dishdashas* were exchanged for guns and the soldiers went off down the road, only to discover that the Americans had not landed and that the explosion had been a blowout in the substation. They returned to where they had exchanged their guns for clothes and said, 'The Americans have not come, so could we have our guns back?'

Sandwiched between the new high-rise buildings in the centre of Kuwait town were the remains of the original marketplace, or souk. Although much smaller than it had originally been, it was a popular place and was seething with life. People went there to look around the gold jewellery shops, to buy from the fruit, vegetable or date section, or just to wander about. It was typical of any Arab marketplace and, in modern parlance, user-friendly. There was a carpet section, where people could be seen examining a Baluchi or Persian rug and, not far away, were *bisht* shops, outside which men sat tap-tapping in gold thread embroidery round the necklines of the garments with a small mallet. This shoulder mantle worn by men (and in some parts of the Arab world by women as well) comes in two versions — heavy winter one and a light, elegant, transparent one worn in the heat of summer over a *dishdasha*. Women's *abat* (silk mantles) were also sold in the souk. Though they now come in many styles, even with embroidery and lace, they are always black. Slightly further away is the *Suq el Hareem* or women's market and for many years the vendors here have all been women, their stalls being in the middle of a wide, shaded street with a variety of shops on either side. They used to sell chickens, herbs, *thob* (embroidered net overdresses) and anything else of interest to women. But the edible items are no longer sold, though *thob* still are, as are white crocheted skullcaps for men, which are now mainly imported from China. Blue 'evil eye' beads can be seen in small dishes, as can pumice stones and loofahs. The women sit there all day ready to bargain with their customers and are always good for an interesting conversation.

The souk had always been an enjoyable place to visit, so I was saddened to hear that parts of it had been burned out and quite badly damaged. Rowa also wanted to pay it a visit and so one morning, with some trepidation at what we might see, we went off in her car to find out exactly what had happened to it. We drove down the long seafront road, which eventually turned off into the centre of town and hence to the souk. For the first time in over 30 years (or probably ever) there was not a single boat to be seen anywhere. The soldiers and their tanks had dug in completely and the entire length of the shore was ready for the expected seaborne landings. That day the sea was grey and cold and the waves were slightly choppy; tangles of barbed wire were strung out along the roads and the edges of the beach like messed-up knitting wool.

In the past Kuwait had been an important seaport, with goods coming from India and China and then going overland as far as Aleppo and, no doubt, elsewhere from there. Until the pearl market finally collapsed in the 1930s, over 12,000 men had in one way or another been associated with the trade. After that, although the graceful big booms (erroneously called dhows by the Europeans) or merchant ships gradually disappeared, smaller cargo boats still crowded the harbour, along with a whole range of modern craft from speedboats to foreign cargo ships. At any time of the day or night one had always been able to see fishing boats, launches and frisky little pleasure craft leaving their trails of foam across the sea. There was a new marina on the seafront and, although we could not stop and stare, it was obvious that many of its craft had disappeared or been sunk.

We parked in the silent dirty souk — the first time in its existence it too was almost empty. The *bisht* market, the women's souk and the carpet section had all been set alight and had fallen in on themselves. A large modern building that had housed some of the gold jewellery shops had been gutted. All that remained were its burned-out hanging shutters, some rubbish and a few 'dead' cars. One part of the souk was still smouldering, so it must only very recently have been set alight; but it looked too dangerous and was in too much of a mess to walk down. We also had to watch our words, for some of the few people walking dismally around were obviously from the *Mukhabarat*.

A brand-new souk had been opened a couple of months before the invasion. Built in the old style by the municipality, with the large wooden doors of each shop opening onto the street and shaded by high covered ceilings, it had been a great architectural success. We decided to go and see what had happened to it, so we shuffled and tripped over the piles of rubbish and picked our way gingerly through squelchy bad-smelling fruit and bits of damp paper that had been thrown out of gaping shop windows. We rounded a corner and saw a sight that typified the horror of what had been taking place.

An empty tiled barrel leant up against a wall in front of us, with a long wooden plank resting on it from the ground. Halfway up the plank lay a surrealistically squashed and flattened cat, with its sightless eyes bulging out like marbles. We squeezed past the barrel, our ankles deep in a mixture of mud and other assorted things that did not bear looking at too closely. In silence we turned the corner and bumped into a woman who gazed at me with a slight grin on her face and said, *sotto voce*, 'A *foreigner*, why is she still staying here?' Moving on quickly after giving her a weak smile, we walked until we eventually reached the new souk. It was still standing. Though looking a little worse for wear, it had neither been burned nor even had its doors removed. With our spirits lifted we stepped briskly into it, intending to have a good look around. But before we were able to move forward more than a couple of feet, a loud voice shouted, '*Memnouh dish dakhil*' (it is forbidden to come inside) and we realized that soldiers, probably officers, had moved into it.

We returned to the car park and drove slowly back towards Jabriya. For some of the way we were stuck behind an army jeep dragging a large rubber boat filled with soldiers wearing sea goggles. I guessed that they might be stationed on Failaka Island and felt a wave of sympathy for the island's 5000 or more inhabitants who had been forcibly thrown out of their houses and then off the island altogether. They had had to come over and live in some of the empty flats on the mainland, while their properties on the island were being completely wrecked and trashed. (Only a couple of the men, who had flatly refused to leave, managed to remain on the island.) I had an opportunity to visit Failaka just after liberation and saw the tremendous damage done to these people's houses because they had been left empty. Here, as elsewhere in Kuwait, piles of ammunition, rockets, mortars, bullets of all sizes and cluster bombs were lying in the grass that had sprung up after the rains. The houses had obviously been 'lived in' — everything was broken, dirty pots and pans had been left lying about and the army had urinated and defecated all over the place. And, as in Kuwait, even private houses had been used as repositories for ammunition and arms.

Living under the Yoke of Oppression

Failaka Island used to be a magical part of Kuwait, and we lived there in the early 1960s for about three months each year because of the archaeological excavations. It is roughly seven miles long and three miles wide. It has a long history of settlement and has been visited for centuries for its various shrines. In 1958 a Danish archaeological expedition investigated its numerous mounds littered with potsherds dating from the dim past to Islamic times. In 1937 the villagers found a stone with 'Soteles, citizen of Athens, and the soldiers... [dedicated this] to Xeus Soteira [the lady saviour]' inscribed on it in Greek. Trading connections with Sumeria and Mohenjodaro (now Pakistan) were uncovered, as were some of the merchants' steatite seal stones for fixing to their merchandise. Similar seals have been found in Pakistan and Bahrain, but there were a lot more of them in Failaka and some seemed to have been made there.

Alexander the Great's commander of the fleet, Nearchos, was ordered to explore the Gulf in 326 BC and he wrote of an island at the head of it that he called Ikaros after the Greek island of the same name. Though more or less continually inhabited, there are records of a dreadful plague on the island in 1841, which drastically reduced the population. But throughout its long history nothing could have been quite as bad as the invasion of 1990.

The soldiers in the large rubber boat stared back at us with interest and, anxious to get past them, we took a turn towards the co-op in Jabriya to see if we could get some bread or a little milk. Kuwaitis were, of course, not allowed any and everyone had to present their ID to the soldier on guard at the entrance, who, if he remembered, might occasionally inspect people's shopping bags as they left. We knew that the manager of that particular co-op, Abu Hani, would slip a few rations into our bags, as he did into those of other Kuwaitis. He trod a difficult and dangerous path between the soldiers and the locals; it was he who had to break up the fights that sometimes developed when supplies like bottled gas came in and people would queue for hours hoping to get some. He also had to try and stop the soldiers helping themselves to food from the shelves, which was a difficult job and one that could easily have led to him being imprisoned or shot. In the end Abu Hani had to go on the run, and for at least a month before liberation he spent each night in a different house. The *Mukhabarat* had of necessity been given a certain amount of the available rations, as well

123

as bribes in exchange for help in freeing some of the many Kuwaiti detainees. Now they began to demand much more and at that time, with supplies so low and no indication of when or if Kuwait might be freed, Abu Hani wanted to conserve as much as possible. It was impossible and unthinkable to say 'no' to (or even to prevaricate with) the *Mukhabarat* and the only thing left to do was to disappear and keep totally out of their way. The co-op's original staff had nearly all left as refugees and it was now being kept open by Kuwaiti volunteers, who did all the lifting and carrying and packing of whatever there was onto the shelves. For people with little or no money a credit system was arranged for the day when, we hoped, Kuwait might be freed.

The KDD (Kuwait Danish Dairy), which supplied milk and dairy products, somehow continued to operate for quite a time after the invasion and helped to control the black market in food. It offered a milk, yoghurt and fruit juice pack for a third of the price charged at the pavement stalls. However, all the equipment at the KDD factory was eventually dismantled and transported (with all the raw materials) to Iraq, for, as readers may remember, the Iraqi government frequently complained that 'the children of Iraq had no milk'. The Government Flour Mills (which supplied free flour to the public for as long as it could) and several other such companies suffered the same fate.

At the end of December we heard that the director of the KDD, Izzat Jaafar, and his son had been arrested and accused of being in contact with the Amir of Kuwait, of subsidizing the Resistance and of giving money to needy citizens. They were taken to prisons in Iraq where both were beaten and tortured — which was especially horrifying given that the older Mr Jaafar was in his eighties. They were released from gaol on 28 March 1991 having been told the night before that they were due to be hanged the next morning. Happily both Mr Jaafar and his son survived and returned to Kuwait and their family.

Most of the time Nadr and I remained in the house. If I took a short walk or went anywhere he stayed behind and vice versa. As the months passed by, however, he went out increasingly frequently to mend water tanks, pumps, air-conditioning, or anything else in which electrical faults occur when there is no maintenance or any spare parts. It was always a worry to be away from the house because one never knew when the army, or *Mukhabarat*, or even looters might choose to appear. However, I did like to get out and see as much as I could so that information about conditions in Kuwait could be passed on to my husband and then on to the Ministry of Defence. My niece Rowa became involved in delivering supplies to people in need and in filling up her car with petrol which was passed on to those unable to obtain it. By December petrol was being rationed and one could only take one tankful from the station. However, because rationing could not be properly organized, it was possible to fill one's tank, siphon it off into another car and then come back for another tankful. Occasionally I was able to accompany her on one of these exploits.

In expectation of sea and air landings the Iraqis now began to spend a great deal of time constructing foxholes and pillboxes and basically digging themselves in. They built absolutely everywhere — on top of and beneath bridges, on the roofs of private houses (by knocking out their windows and filling them in with bricks), against walls and even on the sides of pavements. A pillbox had been constructed in our road by digging beneath the pavement outside a neighbour's house. The water pouring into it when it rained must have nearly drowned its two inhabitants. In any case it was soon abandoned and another one was built upright against the fence. The soldiers became obsessed with these shelters from which to shoot, and on one of the days when I went with Rowa on her petrol rounds we could see the army building them everywhere. One pillbox became quite famous for it had obviously been painstakingly constructed and was rather nicely whitewashed. As we drove slowly past it, we saw an officer walk up to the two men who were, so we thought, putting the finishing touches to it. He did not seem to be pleased and we imagined he might be lecturing them and saying, 'You fools, these are meant to be camouflaged.' On passing the now completed pillbox at the beginning of the bridge a few days later, it was decorated all over with large bilious green dots. A big photograph of Saddam was in place at the entrance surrounded by some plastic roses. We did not think that these shelters would be much use against bombing by B52s, but no doubt the Iraqis (and for that matter everyone else) were expecting sea attacks and parachute landings.

On that same journey we ran into a couple of road checks at which soldiers were handing out free copies of the Iraqi Ba'ath Party propaganda newspaper, *Al Nida'a* (The Call), now being produced from the premises of a prominent Kuwaiti printing press and newspaper, *Al Qabas*. All other printing presses had been dismantled and their machinery taken to Iraq. *Al Nida'a* was highly unpopular in Kuwait. As well as being exceedingly boring, for it relayed and publicized endless speeches by Saddam, it tried to undermine Kuwaiti patriotism and loyalty to the ruling family and circulated lies about the situation in Kuwait. It was distributed and sold well in Jordan, but in Kuwait it had to be given away free. Yet Kuwaitis were eventually forced to read it to find out the latest rules and regulations, which the paper carried every day. Practically the entire staff of *Al Qabas*, which included both Kuwaiti and expatriate Arab journalists, either moved house or left the country to avoid having to cooperate in its printing. *Al Nida'a* 'died' a dishonourable death shortly before liberation; the last of the printing presses were taken away and the building was ransacked and burned.

More for the sake of getting out of the house than anything else and because we needed, if possible, to get some bread and milk, Rowa and I set off once more to the Jabriya co-op. Each time we went there the shelves seemed to contain less and less of anything that could be eaten. The freezers had long been empty and it was not hard to memorize what remained. I joined a queue for three flaps of breads and a small carton of milk and, that completed, went off to find Rowa in front of a jar of Vaseline she was wondering if she could afford.

I said to her in Arabic, 'What is that?' and she made some reply in English. At that point we both simultaneously noticed a drab man with hard eyes glowering at us. A couple of feet away and half round the corner of a shelf, he picked up a bottle of shampoo and put it down again, his eyes never leaving us, flickering from one to the other. There was no doubt about it. He was in the *Mukhabarat* and viewed us as suspicious characters.

It should not be thought that we felt light-hearted or frivolous about being watched by the *Mukhabarat*; it was not a laughing matter at all and we were both horrified and frightened. But it was difficult to repress a grin at so obvious a stereotype. Wherever we moved he was around the corner, by a shelf or staring into the empty freezers. At one point all three of us were lined up together gazing earnestly at packets of washing soap. Having bought what little we could we decided to leave and try to shake him off that way. While queuing to pay at the tills, he was the sixth person behind us. I greeted Mrs Raj, the wife of the British vice-consul, who was working there as a volunteer and then, clutching our bags, we walked out to the car. We knew we had to shake him off before either of us went home. Keaton had not yet been released and Abu Ali lived down the road not far from us in the same block of flats as Rowa. They were hiding a Kuwaiti intelligence officer friend of theirs and neither of us could afford to attract any attention. The flats already seemed to be being watched and on a couple of occasions there had been visits from members of the *Mukhabarat* claiming to be looking for a place to rent.

Slowly, to show we were not acting in a suspicious manner, we put our few bags in the back seat, got into the car and drove away, watching him pull out behind and start tailing us at a respectable distance. We turned round a corner, moved a little faster and cut into a short street. He was coming down on the other side of the road. We gave no indication that we knew he was following and neither did he acknowledge us. This continued for some time. We turned into side streets, went behind into even smaller ones and still he appeared. As we turned down into a long wide double carriageway we could see his car on the other side at the bottom. Rowa sighed and remarked that we had better let him know that we knew what he was up to. As the cars drew parallel we would wave to him. Slowing down slightly we both leaned forward smiling and waved to him graciously. However gross a person might be, Arab manners are not easily forgotten. Both his hands were resting on the wheel and as we waved courteously, he lifted one off in greeting, then realizing halfway through the incongruity of his gesture, he let his hand slip slowly back onto the wheel. It instantly reminded us both of a popular advertisement in which an extra-terrestrial being (ET) tries to make a six-million-dollar telephone call home and his hand slides slowly down the wall in disappointment at the impossible price.

For a short while we seemed to have lost him, but just as we prepared to make a rush for our houses, there he was again, this time in disguise. He had put on a pair of dark glasses, presumably so that we would not recognize him. In the end, unable to shake him off, we slipped into the car park of a busy private hospital, which was being much used by Kuwaitis now that they were no longer allowed to receive free treatment at the government hospitals. It was a busy time of the morning. We looked around to see if his car was in the vicinity and then hurried across the road to go inside the main entrance and mingle with the crowds. There we remained for about an hour. Now and again we saw friends waiting for treatment — one of them was expecting a baby. There were few medical facilities available by then but at least she would be able to have her child in a relatively safe place. Rowa lived behind the hospital so she left her car in the car park. But my house was further down the road, so I walked back through side streets watching out for any cars like the one we had succeeded in shaking off. Thankfully we never saw the man again.

Everyone was aware (and some only too well aware) that many Kuwaitis had been picked up and imprisoned, that this had been going on since the first day of the invasion and that the Iraqis had imposed an information blackout on their whereabouts for at least the first three months of the occupation. One afternoon, as I was climbing the stairs to Rowa's flat for a quick cup of tea, one of her friends arrived who had just heard that her brother, whom she had thought was safely in Bahrain was actually a prisoner of war in the Ba'aqouba POW camp just outside Baghdad. She had been told that it was now possible for relatives to drive up and visit the detainees. These visits had been facilitated by a Kuwaiti, Mr Mahmoud Qabazard, who had been one of the people trying to find out what had happened to prisoners ever since his own officer son had been taken prisoner on the first day of the invasion. The visits had been made possible through an Iraqi (a retired senior Ba'ath Party official) who used his influence to shift some of the men from a prison in Mosul in the north to the Baghdad gaol. This was at a cost of ID 100,000, four Chevrolet saloons and two trucks — and all for the official's personal use.

Mr Qabazard's other son, Ahmad Qabazard, had been captured, tortured and finally shot outside his house, where his body was left lying for a couple of days in the usual manner. Ahmad, who served with the Ministry of Defence VIP protection unit, had been outside the country at the time of the invasion. He determined that he would re-enter Kuwait and fight for the Resistance. He came over the border in the third week of the occupation disguised as a shepherd and joined a group under the leadership of Colonel Mahmoud Al Dosari, which became engaged in blowing up ammunition trucks and other such demolition jobs. After his capture he was tortured most brutally in an attempt to get him to reveal the names of the other people in his group, but he never did.

We were given a personal account of the last part of his story one afternoon in early September when my neighbour, Mrs Abu Huntash, was rung up by an hysterically weeping Sri Lankan maid who lived opposite Ahmad Qabazard's villa. Her employers were out of the country on holiday and she was taking care of the house. Hearing the whine of police car sirens she went to the window overlooking the street and saw Iraqi police cars and an army truck with armed soldiers draw up at the house opposite. According to the maid, Ahmad was pulled out of the car and, by now unable to stand, had been supported on either side by two men. The police officer turned and said something to him, Ahmad managed to lift his head up and spat in his face, whereupon he was shot dead. The army then proceeded first to loot the house then to RPG (rocket-propelled grenade) it, which set it ablaze. Like the Deshti house near us it went up with a roar and for a while it seemed quite possible that the other houses might also catch fire. The police cars drove away leaving the body lying in the road where it was eventually picked up by Ahmad's father and taken to the cemetery for burial. The maid packed her bags and came over to stay in Mrs Abu Huntash's house until she was able to leave Kuwait.

Now that relatives had permission to visit their kin in the various Iraqi gaols, they began to prepare for the long drive. We all helped them pack boxes with warm *dishdashas*, socks, shoes, shaving kits and anything else we could think of that could possibly be of use. A great many of the prisoners had been wearing summer clothes when they were picked up and, as we found out later, had to survive in them without any change. As those who survived repeated time and time again, conditions were like those of a concentration camp, with chronic overcrowding, beatings, torture and such poor food that some of them lost as much as 20 kilos of weight in a couple of months. The guards were open to bribery if there was anything with which to bribe them. I believe it was in the prison just outside Baghdad (which held over 600 Kuwaitis) that, to the amazement of their guards, the inmates organized themselves along disciplined army lines and shared out all their food and clothing.

It was actually quite dangerous to make these visits. Not only might the relatives be made to wait some time before being allowed to see their relatives, but it was quite possible that the visiting family (men, women and children) would find themselves behind bars as well. Whole families, and there were quite a number of our pupils among them, found themselves in prisons all over Iraq for all kinds of reasons.

One 12-year-old wrote in our 1991/2 yearbook that his father had been arrested for failing to change his ID or car numberplates. 'They came to our house, took KD 4000 and stole our car.' The rest of the family were then arrested and taken to Basra prison where, without water or food, many people began to suffer from disease and some died. The family was put in a room filled with women and children aged between six months and 12 years. He wrote that, 'The Iraqi policeman came into the room and started to shout at us and my mother told them I was 10 years old and so I was not taken away.' They were allowed to see the men every Friday and water was sold to them by their guards for 10 dinars a bucket. They could hear men and women crying and screaming every night. This particular family was moved from Basra gaol to Baghdad and then back again in time for the bombing of Basra by the Allies. The soldiers locked them in a bus before running away to hide. When some soldiers returned to pick up the bus after the raid, they were taken back to Basra gaol and put in a cell with other people. There they remained until 2 March, when their family was released by the 'Iraqi rebels who hated Saddam Hussein and came and killed half the policemen and opened the doors for us and we walked from Basra to the Kuwait border, where a Kuwaiti family came and took us in their car back to Kuwait.'

As some of these detainees began to return after the liberation an exhibition was organized to show what life had been like in prison. Apart from some dreadful photographs of the victims of torture, which had been taken secretly and kept hidden by those who had buried some of the dead, there was an extensive display of various practical or essential objects that the prisoners had made in their cells. Included among the exhibits were waistcoats and jackets made from bits of blanket and cast-off material, footwear embroidered with small patterns in chain and running stitch, patriotic and religious carvings in stone picked from the ground. By some of those who had managed to obtain paper and pencil there were passages from the Holy Koran in surprisingly fine script considering the circumstances. There were even a few small waistcoats and *dishdashas*, though it is not known whether these were made for children in prison, or in the hopes that release would come sooner or later.

Although Kuwaitis were the main target for humiliation and cruelty, other nationalities, quite aside from the hostages and refugees, did not escape ill treatment. One particular case remains in my memory of an Indian who went to a police station to retrieve his car book that had been taken away during a road check. Along with about 15 other people he had been told to pick up his book and the car the next day. Half the people with him refused to go on the grounds that it was too risky, but this man decided to go and, to show he was a family man and therefore needed his car, he took his 10-year-old daughter with him. His wife and younger child remained behind in their flat. All those from that group, including the man and his daughter, were arrested and taken to Basra gaol. After some time in prison the authorities released the child — she was literally put outside the prison gates and told to walk back to Kuwait over some 150 kilometres of arid, gravel-covered countryside. She apparently did just that, fortunately in the company of a Kuwaiti family who had found themselves in the same situation.

At no time did life during the occupation proceed on an even keel. There were periods when rumours one longed to believe caused short-lived bursts of hope and optimism. There were also one or two occasions, each lasting for about 10 days, when really dark despair swept through everybody in Kuwait. It was barely possible to tolerate another minute of the anxiety and apprehension. Some spoke of trying to leave and some went, only to have their menfolk taken and imprisoned by the Iraqis on the border. They all had to part with their IDs and various papers, as well as suffer other humiliations. Those who remained in Kuwait sank into depressions and, depending on their personalities, either walked around like zombies or moaned incessantly. The slightly less despondent supported the ones who were completely down, and people threatening to leave were exhorted to hold out a little longer. Gradually the particularly bad days passed. Though never quite lifting, the cloud eased a bit and somehow people managed to continue to exist one day at a time.

To people in Kuwait, it was becoming steadily more apparent that the Iraqis wished (or perhaps with their penchant for mental torture intended us to think they wished) to practise a scorched-earth policy of removing both the people of Kuwait and its buildings. Everyone felt that the Allied Forces in Saudi Arabia were being built up too slowly. Newspaper reports in 1992 maintained that the number of troops deployed in Kuwait was lower than previously estimated. Judging from what we could see, this seemed unlikely. Our school (except towards the end) housed about 800 men, the Iranian school perhaps 400 and the nearby government schools a similar number to our school. In addition, soldiers were deployed in the French and Chinese embassies and in many of the surrounding empty houses and all this in an area of approximately 1000 square metres. They were deployed all over the desert, in the numerous government schools, along the beaches and in hundreds of vacated and empty houses. Even a rapid estimate adds up to a considerable number of men. Of course when it comes to professionals that is a different matter.

Everyone realized that if it came to street or house-to-house fighting the population would suffer greatly, particularly since very few people had much in the way of arms. I developed a mild obsession about the stout, brass-decorated entrance next door and would stand staring at it and imagining hammering more teak planks across the ones already there and... Instead I dragged two heavy brass containers against it and as far as possible barricaded any other doors. I knew perfectly well that nothing stood a chance against RPGs and even going down into the basement would not save our lives. Nevertheless we all longed to see an American marine or desert rat coming up the street and we were all prepared to sneak round corners with stout sticks trying to knock out Iraqi soldiers or do what little we could to help the liberation.

On 6 December, quite unexpectedly, Iraq announced that all hostages and people in hiding were free to leave Iraq and Kuwait and return to their countries. Keaton heard the news on the radio and we all chattered excitedly for a time, for no one was quite sure exactly how to come out of hiding. Most people were very cautious, for they now knew how easily the Iraqis could change their minds and suspected that this might even be a ploy to capture everyone. Not surprisingly, a few of the men were so overwhelmed and excited that they had to be restrained from rushing out to take a walk or from going to see what had happened in their offices. Keaton sensibly waited for instructions from the American Embassy before taking the next step. He did, however, pack what little he had left and then wondered what he would wear. He had worn Arab clothing throughout his time in hiding and had grown a beard, which he did not intend to remove at that moment. We all scuffled around trying to find a large pair of jeans and a T-shirt, for Keaton was a tall man. He had lost a great deal of weight during his four months of incarceration, which was partly intentional and partly because of the shortage of food. He was packed and ready to move when Barbara Bodine rang from the American Embassy a day after the news of the release to tell us what to do and whom to contact. For some reason the Iraqis were feeling magnanimous and, on orders from Baghdad and out of the blue, some food supplies were sent in to the embassy. Barbara said she had never before realized how good a tangerine could taste. Her colleague commented that when they celebrated the news of the releases with a can of Pepsi, it too tasted marvellous. Our friend Bill also rang from his hiding place and promised to pass by and have a cup of tea. He was advised against it, though, on the grounds that the Iraqis might well be watching to find out who had been hiding and feeding all those people.

On the evening of 8 December Keaton, still bearded but clad in jeans and T-shirt, was ready to leave to spend his last night in a flat about a mile away. We prepared to go once more into our 'spy' routine. Still using the Suzuki we drove casually past the block of flats where we assumed Keaton had to be dropped off. This time we got it right and once it was dark we all went together, looking around carefully to see that no one was watching when we came to a stop near the gate. He slipped out of the car with his few possessions and like a ghost disappeared through the open door to freedom. In the early morning the men were taken by bus to the airport and from there flown to Baghdad. Finally the men reached their homes in America or Britain, nervous and exhausted after their bizarre and unforgettable experiences.

Although we were all delighted that the men were able to leave, it was impossible to escape the feeling of total isolation that swept over us. Even embassy personnel were going to be leaving, though the embassy itself was not considered shut down, merely unstaffed for the time being. Our last contact with western civilization seemed to be disappearing — there had been such a tremendous feeling of fellow-ship with the people in hiding. Indeed, quite a number were torn between remaining and going. Some wanted to show their solidarity with the Kuwaitis, but equally their families expected them to return. The British ambassador and his consul, Larry Banks, would, as they put it, 'have preferred to see it through to the end'. This gave me a little comfort, for it showed that they at least thought that Kuwait would eventually be free.

A day or so after the men in hiding had gone, Rowa and I drove to Salmiya to collect some frozen food from a colleague, who was also leaving Kuwait, and to visit the Sultan Centre to try and buy a torch and batteries for when the electricity went out, as we realized it inevitably would.

The suburb of Salmiya lying along the seashore some eight miles from Kuwait town had, 40 years before, been a village with a mosque, some houses and a few sheikhly residences. Because the climate was considered favourable the village started to develop into a township. In 1940, in *Sons of Sindbad*, the sailor, Alan Villiers wrote about his experiences of pearl ships and of sailing with Arab cargo in the Gulf. He found then that 'this amazing place Kuwait' was a city and had a seafront that never ceased to interest him. He mentions living in 1939 with his friends the Al Hamads at their walled country house by the beach in Dimnah (now Salmiya). He describes how they slept on the sand with the sound of the surf breaking on the shore and the brilliant stars shining overhead. As the Al Hamads were shipowners, many of their *nakhodas* (captains) would walk the eight miles from the town to visit them, all of which was of great interest to Alan Villiers. The Al Hamads' modern houses are still near the seashore and many members of the family remained in Kuwait throughout the occupation. The Iraqis ordered them to leave their houses during the air war, but they refused to do so, saying that the Iraqis could shoot them if they wished, but they would not leave.

Over the years Salmiya became a sprawling, somewhat graceless, yet lively, shopping and residential centre. It acquired schools, clinics, shopping complexes (including the Sultan Centre) and a cinema. Until the days of the video the cinema had thrived, with Thursday evenings being family evenings and an occasion to chew nuts, popcorn and an astonishing variety of other foods. With video the magic of the cinema faded, though a few people still continued to go to it. On the large roundabout leading to the cinema now stood a giant portrait of Saddam Hussein. Each night it was shot to pieces by Kuwaitis until in the end (and on this particular day when we passed it) it was guarded from all angles by about eight heavily armed and somewhat nervous-looking soldiers.

Salmiya was now a bleak, garbage-strewn, disorderly mess. A ghost town feeling of decay was already creeping in. The gold souk was barred and bolted and its steel shutters pulled down. Walking amongst people with their strained, joyless faces and then staring across the road, I could see a trio of soldiers squatting down and trying to prise apart the bars of the shutters of a shop. Amidst the rubbish on the pavements stood the usual street market vendors and at every corner there lounged what were obviously members of the *Mukhabarat* in their dark glasses. We collected the food from our friend and then went as fast as possible to the Sultan Centre. As elsewhere, its shelves were half empty, its top floor reached by escalators had been closed off and the once attractive vegetable section with its different coloured peppers had gone. Rowa and I gazed sadly in the direction of the deserted café where we had chatted over so many cappuccinos. We saw a few friends wandering around like us and shared our sense of gloom with them, feeling slightly better for having done so. Then slowly we drove back along the dangerous roads to our houses.

The standard of driving in Kuwait had never been high, but it had now taken a turn for the worse. Some traffic lights had been stolen and others had fused or somehow failed through lack of maintenance. From the start no rules or regulations were observed. Bits of blown-up army vehicles and shattered cars were scattered across the roads and potholes were beginning to appear as a result of all the tanks and heavy lorries constantly rolling along them. Our brief visit had been a more than usually depressing one. Each time I ventured out Kuwait looked more dilapidated. The Iraqis' total disinterest in preserving even a façade of maintenance or cleanliness was one of the reasons why people felt that a scorched-earth policy was eventually intended. And many people decided to remain in Kuwait precisely because of the growing feeling that the Iraqis wanted to turn as many Kuwaitis as possible into dispossessed refugees.

There were periods when I considered it possible to take short walks away from my house in the afternoons. Usually I went out when the young men played a little football, though as the months went by they went out less and less and finally had to give up altogether. Kuwait had never really been a place for walking, but over the past few years paths had been laid out in each district and were much used for jogging or strolling. The long seafront had been a favourite venue for fishing, running or just sitting out in the fresh air drinking a cup of coffee in a café. Along the seafront, between the British and American embassies, stands the symbol of modern Kuwait — three stylish and spectacular water towers, or pinnacles, one with a revolving restaurant near the top. Besides taking a daily look to see if Kathem had disappeared, I would climb up onto the roof to see if the towers were still standing. They had been shot at and all their glass had been broken, but being constructed of tough, solid concrete, they did somehow survive.

During Ramadan (the month of fasting) my older son, Ziad, would often accompany me on a short walk for about an hour before the fast broke to look at any new houses being built. It was amazing how distinct an atmosphere even a short section of street could emanate. One day in the middle of December, noticing that the boys were outside playing football, I decided to go out and have a look around. I walked down side roads to avoid any sight of a uniform and occasionally stopped to chat to people who had cautiously decided to sit out on their doorsteps. Quite a few had planted tomatoes and lettuces to help with their food problems and some even had a goat or sheep to eat the leftovers. Once or twice I passed a giant trailer parked outside a block of flats or an empty house and guessed, by the suspicious and slightly guilty glances cast in my direction, that all the contents were being removed. As I came round the corner of another large square block of flats I saw prayers for protection pasted up on all the gates. They were later torn down, probably by soldiers, and strewn all over the street.

At the end of that road there was an overflowing and pungent rubbish skip and, as I came nearer, it swelled and heaved like a living entity. Scores of huge-eyed, skinny cats squirmed out and ran onto the road causing me to mutter, 'Puss, puss, poor things, never mind.' It reminded me of one of my grandmothers, who had gone out each day during the Blitz in London to feed and rescue 'bombed-out' cats. I passed a ground-floor flat with all its doors swinging open and items of underwear, a white slip, a pair of briefs and some shoes tumbling into the yard. Through the window I could see a long bookshelf of untouched books though the rest of the room was a shambles. I longed to take a look at the books, and see what the owners had read, but did not dare to stop.

Crossing the main road by the Jabriya police station and keeping well away from it, I walked into a complex of fairly new and recently completed houses. Down one road was a blue Suzuki and two men, who were probably up to no good as they seemed to be breaking and entering. Suddenly I realized that most of the houses had their windows bricked in and that the Iraqi Army was heavily entrenched in there. I could hardly wait to get away for it was no place to be wandering about, but I could not run out for that would surely be suspicious and attract attention.

I decided to move slowly out towards the main road again and had just crossed a street when I heard shouting behind me. Pretending not to have heard it, I moved slowly up the slight incline to try and get out of sight and maybe into an empty garden. A couple of feet further on, a jeep roared up behind me with four bad-tempered-looking soldiers seated in it.

As they piled out, one of them (presumably an officer) shouted, 'Why are you walking in there? It's *memnouh*' (forbidden). Hearing him say the word *memnouh* reminded me of the house search when the officer told us he had come to give us our 'freedom' and a great surge of indignation and fury swept over me. *Freedom*! We were all barely able to walk about and might quite likely die in a number of unpleasant ways, everyone was fearful for their lives, people were having their houses set aflame, others were being taken to gaol for nothing. Some freedom. The officer repeated harshly, 'It's forbidden to walk or go in there.'

Temper unwisely overcoming caution I shouted back, 'I thought you had come to give us our freedom. Why shouldn't I walk? I like to walk, I'm free to walk, don't we have freedom to do anything any more?' That at least was the intention, but in sheer rage my Arabic totally fell apart, words poured out, but through the haze of temper even I could only understand one word I had said — '*hurriyeti*' (my

137

freedom). For the pause of an indrawn breath the four men stepped backwards in horror, their faces amazed and wondering what these appalling words were that might be Arabic. The officer asked, 'Where were you born?' In Arabic that can mean 'What nationality are you?' Knowing I had been incredibly silly I answered truthfully and more politely that I had been born in Brazil. Again the man repeated, 'It's forbidden to walk over there,' and, on looking over in the direction of the half-finished houses, I realized that this was certainly no place to be wandering around, so more calmly I said, 'I am sorry, I did not know that. I will not walk there again.'

They demanded to see my ID, which I produced with an inward sigh of relief that I was not carrying my camera, which I sometimes did. They stared at the ID and by way of forestalling questions I said I was married to a Kuwaiti and had lived in Kuwait for many years. The officer handed back the card, still repeating it was forbidden to walk over there. Once more I apologized and with a nasty look they all climbed back into the jeep and moved away. I slowly continued along the road, somewhat shaken and aware that I had had a very lucky escape.

That evening a relative, who was in the Resistance and had been involved in the hiding of and caring for a number of westerners, dropped by to see how we were. While alone in his house a few nights before he had heard rustling and movement in the rooms below. He went quietly downstairs and caught a soldier in the act of stealing. He threatened to hand the man over to the authorities as it was 'forbidden to steal' and was begged by the trembling, frightened man to let him go as otherwise he would be shot. This was probably true, for the Iraqis would be happy to use the mere soldier to show the now suspicious world how much the authorities disapproved of theft. Our relative, knowing that what the man said was probably true, told the soldier to go and not come back again.

Nadr had been going round trying to inspect the water tanks and electricity, for the pressure had become unreliable towards the end of December and, in any case, there had been no official maintenance since the start of the invasion. Part of my childhood was spent in the Cape Verde islands, where there had been a shortage of water. This was said to have been caused by over 400 years of cutting down trees and leaving much of the land waste. It did not rain there often, but when it did it poured down. Most of the population were enchanted by this and would run outside in a state of undress to enjoy the rare pleasure. My island nanny had told me the story of Noah and the flood, and the first time I saw huge heavy drops gathering into puddles I thought Noah's flood had come again and we would all drown. In those early days there was no electricity and cleaning the glass of the lamps and trimming their wicks was part of the daily routine. Of all the modern benefits, water and electricity are the ones I appreciate most and the ones I most feared losing. There is no doubt that had the water and electricity failed during the first weeks of the invasion many more people would have died.

Very early in the morning of 3 August, the second day of the invasion, I woke with a start, for the reflection of the grille made by the mosque light shining through the window had gone and it was pitch black. The electricity had failed and the whole area was in darkness. I wandered round the house for a while, trying not to think what it would be like without electricity and (worse in that heat) water. I decided not to wake anyone up; they would know soon enough when the air grew hotter and stuffier. Mentally preparing myself for the worst I went back to the bedroom and fell into an uneasy sleep. When I woke up again the electricity was on once more and I could hear the soft hum of the air-conditioning and the refrigerator in the background. As no one was aware of what had happened, had it been a dream? Had the electricity really cut out? I still do not know.

When Nadr returned from working on the water tanks he would sit awhile on the outside steps before going on to his next job. The cat, Dali, a half-Persian with an uncertain temperament made worse by the prevailing conditions, would sit beside him purring slightly. One afternoon Nadr stooped to stroke the cat's head and Dali, apparently caught unawares, leapt forward with claws out and teeth digging into Nadr's hand. It took a minute or two to persuade him to loosen his grip and to shake him off. The cuts were deep and had to be cleaned and wiped with disinfectant. But within a few hours Nadr's temperature began to rise, the hand to swell and his head to throb unbearably. Luckily for us one of Rowa's friends managed to obtain some penicillin tablets and the swelling and temperature began to go down. This was no time to need treatment of any kind. My memory of the first

139

five months of the occupation is of feeling basically healthy and even losing some unwanted weight. According to my journal, however, this was not the case, for on a number of occasions I suffered attacks of giddiness and nausea, along with mysterious swellings of the fingers and joints. As there was little that could be done about it, it was just ignored and forgotten.

As December came to an end the news from the *diwaniyas* (special sitting rooms where men congregate to discuss anything and everything) was that Kuwaitis would soon not even be allowed inside a co-op unless they had changed their nationality. A new date for the change had been set for the middle of January 1991. Ever-increasing numbers of arrests were being made in the *diwaniyas*, with men being taken to prison on numerous flimsy charges. With a dumbfounded expression on her face, one of Rowa's friends told her that the machinery from their potato crisp factory had been removed to Iraq on the grounds that, 'It was forbidden to make crisps, and nobody wanted them anyhow, so the machinery was no longer needed,' which seemed an original kind of logic.

We continued to watch some of the television programmes and from them learned that Saddam Hussein had paid another visit to the troops inside Kuwait and had awarded his officers a rise of ID 50. The BBC reported a rise for the entire army, which did not seem to be true because the ordinary soldiers at least denied any knowledge of the rise. At a private hospital trying to buy some medicine, Abu Yaseen was approached by the soldier on guard duty at the gates for cigarettes and he asked him if they had been awarded any kind of pay rise. The soldiers must have been listening to foreign Arab stations on their stolen radios, for the man remarked resentfully that *they* were given little food, while the American Army even had 'hamburrrgers and chippes'. For once no informers seemed to be in evidence and the soldier went on to comment sadly that if war broke out he felt that this time he would be killed, and then who would support his wife and child, for all his brothers were dead, wiped out in the Iraq–Iran war. He himself had been a prisoner at the beginning of that war and had hardly seen his now 10-year-old son.

As he spoke other Kuwaitis had been coming in and stopping to listen. With tears in his eyes he said that he had been released from Iran a few weeks before August 1990 and had spent a mere month in his village before being ordered back into the army. Such was his apparent sadness that the Kuwaitis, who had had no intention of parting with their cigarettes, which were now expensive and difficult to get hold of, dug into their pockets and gave him everything they could find. The story might have been play-acting on the soldier's part, but it did have a ring of truth to it.

Iraq had now been given until 15 January 1991 to begin its withdrawal from Kuwait. The two weeks before the air war were characterized by an almost eerie silence, a feeling of waiting, with very little shooting, at least around us, seeming to take place. The talks in Geneva between the US secretary of state, James Baker, and the Iraqi foreign minister, Tareq Aziz, had failed and it looked to us as if the Iraqis had merely been using them as a way of playing for time. The troops were dug in along the entire seafront and on the bare land in front of the school there was a little buzz of activity, with men energetically digging trenches and bunkers. The wall surrounding a small building just up the road from the school had gradually lost most of its bricks, until all that remained were its supporting pillars and tottery blocks of wired cement on the top struggling to hold the original shape together. At opposite ends of the square were two locked gates, which under different circumstances might have been seen as a form of modern art.

We heard that the Iraqis had begun to move their administration out of Kuwait and that those who occupied flats had been ordered to return to Iraq. People with ration cards were told to use them up before 10 January. We heard that something like 100,000 ration books had been issued to non-Kuwaitis but only 10 or 12 to Kuwaiti families. Certainly I knew of no one with such a card. We still hoped that with all the pressure on Iraq the army might withdraw peacefully, but reluctantly one had to be honest and recognize that there was absolutely no indication that the army was leaving. Rather, to our amazement, it increasingly appeared that it was preparing to stay and fight.

While soldiers dug more trenches, removed bricks from pavements and walls and blocked in more windows all over Kuwait, everyone else placed tape across their windows and prepared their basements for the expected bombing. They equipped them with water, blankets and whatever food they could manage to find and, as a precaution against chemical warfare, either via warheads or simply at street level, securely taped over their air-conditioning outlets. It was very strongly rumoured that the Iraqi governor, Ali Hassan Al Majeed, was waiting for permission from a higher authority to embark on just such a programme. We gave a door key to our neighbours, for they had no basement, while Abu Ali, Rowa and her mother decided that if the worst came to the worst they would go over to the hospital basement opposite them. Home-made flags bearing the red crescent and cross fluttered over the roof and on the flagstaffs of the hospital. One of them carried a large H for hospital.

Nobody wanted to use their basements unless it was absolutely necessary, for they knew that their property would be looted even while bombing was in progress. In the director's house it was obvious that the oven and microwave had been on the list for removal, for they were found pushed near to the kitchen door. Microwave ovens seem to have been popular in Iraq, despite the fact that many villages lacked electricity and people would not have known how to operate them. An unpleasant character from the Red Berets at the Iranian school had been roving around with a truck full of soldiers 'collecting' things. He had been demanding a microwave oven for some time, but before he could obtain one he went on a short leave to Iraq, along with two box air-conditioners he had 'collected' from somewhere and leaving orders that a microwave should be found for him. He asked Abu Ali to try and obtain one for him and, to keep him quiet, Abu Ali had wearily said that if and when one could be found he could have it. On his return from his leave in Hilla (old Babylon) in Iraq he reappeared at Abu Ali's back door. Sulkily demanding *his* oven, he craned his head past Abu Ali (who was blocking the door), saw their oven and said, 'That's mine!' Abu Ali remarked that it did not belong to him and would he please wait until one had been found. In the end his regiment was, we thought, transferred to Ahmadi and he was never heard from again.

There had been periodic curfews throughout the five months since the invasion, especially at night, but now they were to be more rigorously enforced. But the invaders appeared unable to agree over whether there was a curfew at all. Soldiers at road checks maintained there was one, those at the Jabriya police station denied it. It did not matter that much, however, for most people remained in their houses after dark, while those who went out shooting soldiers or portraits of Saddam Hussein would have gone out anyway.

On Tuesday 15 January 1991 the weather was sunny but surprisingly cold, as it so often can be at that time of year. Heavy rain fell at intervals and some of the hapless *jindis* in their dugouts must have nearly drowned as the water oozed in. The unlamented propaganda newspaper *Al Nida'a* had ceased to operate and, along with all its remaining press machinery, had been taken off to Iraq. The water pressure and electricity were failing. What the population wanted (and by then perhaps even the soldiers, who did not understand what was going to happen) was action. Even being killed in street fighting or by bombing was better than living under the Iraqi regime. We waited amid a deadly silence, our stomachs churning; we were on the brink of we knew not what.

PART III

Liberation
17 January to 26 February 1991

9

Liberation

SHORTLY before 3.00 a.m. on the morning of Thursday 17 January, Nadr woke me up. The BBC had interrupted its programme to go over to its reporters in Baghdad because the Iraqi capital was under air attack from the Allied forces. I leapt out of bed with a shriek of delight and threw on some clothes, even though I was only going to watch the television. Some idea of the relief we all felt is evident in an interview later given to an American newspaper by a 10-year-old pupil from our school called Abeer. She said, 'In Arabic there is a word *ahlan*. It means welcome. So when you hear bombs happening, you say *ahlan*.'

Outside flares were going up into the sky and, far in the distance, we could hear what sounded like heavy guns firing. I later read that the BBC and CNN (the American Cable News Network that became internationally known during the Gulf crisis) correspondents in Baghdad had been criticized for describing the air battles and the flares rising into the sky as if they had been a fireworks display, but in truth it did look exactly like that. Directly outside us there was some gunfire and shouting, but it was impossible to tell whether it was *Jesh Sha'abi* (the People's Army) nervously shooting at its own feet, people rejoicing at the news, or something else.

We rang up everyone we could think of, but like us, they were all glued to their televisions. We later heard that my daughter, Nur, had been lying in bed in England with her radio earphones plugged in when the announcer broke into a programme to say that the Allies were bombing Baghdad. She rang her father, who like everyone else had become permanently attached to the radio, but he had already heard the news and was now in front of the television. He rang friends in Jordan who (along with some Jordanian intellectuals) were sympathetic to Kuwait and had not supported Iraq's actions. The propaganda machine in Jordan had had virtually nothing to say about events in Kuwait so many people there were very shocked at the turn events had taken. My friend Beverley, who lives in Bath, tore upstairs on hearing the news to wake her daughters, Lee Anne and Paula, so that they could watch the news coverage. Nadr's wife, Denise, who had given birth to a baby girl two weeks before, wept with relief that at last something was beginning to happen. My eldest son, Ziad, shortly to volunteer as an interpreter in the British Army, and his wife Leila, were also transfixed in front of their television. Probably half the people of Britain, Kuwait and elsewhere were sitting in front of their boxes watching President Bush announce the start of the air war and the spectacular bombing of Baghdad.

Thursday 17 January 1991
Having been up all night as usual, Nadr shook me awake at about 2.30 a.m. to say that President Bush had made a short and to the point speech to announce the start of the air war. I dressed quickly, quite why I do not know seeing that I was only going to another room, but somehow the importance of the occasion seemed to demand it. We could hear what might have been heavy gunfire in the far distance, but it had been raining steadily the day before, so it could have been the rumblings of the ponderous thunder that sometimes rolls around the skies over the desert and sends out spectacular stabs of lightening to pierce the sand. There were red flares shooting up in the sky around us and outbursts of gunfire now and again. We sat in front of the TV (wrapped in any blankets we could find because it was cold) with our eyes fixed on the screen. The sky was alive with tracer flares (the background a pulsating orange-red from the multiple explosions) and droning with the rumble of aircraft. It may not be a nice thing to think but we felt that Iraq deserved what it was getting, especially considering what it had done to Kuwait. As I write this the electricity is flickering and the water pressure is definitely going to present quite a problem.

We remained near the television with the radio balanced alongside it for most of the day. Not only did we hear the big guns booming in the distance, but it also began to rain again and the roar of the guns got mixed up with the crash of thunder. I took a short walk down the road, but not too far down because I could neither go near to the occupied Iranian school at the end, nor pass too close to our own school, and anyway very few people seemed to be out and about.

Friday 18 January 1991
Nadr woke me again to say that Iraq had fired Scud missiles at Israel and at Dhahran in Saudi Arabia. There were more television shots of Baghdad being bombed, this time with planes flying at high altitudes and precision bombing the Ministry of Defence — quite incredible!

The early-morning prayer was called against a background of ferocious thuds and firing and this more or less continued until later in the morning. Again it was very cloudy and poured with rain, which had me worrying about the possibility of a leakage both next door and upstairs where the costume cupboards are. I kept going upstairs, opening the doors and feeling around the dresses to see if any water had seeped in. Our glass roof over the top storage area leaks badly every time the rains begin. However often the joints are sealed the scorching heat of summer causes them to shrink. We had put two ladders on either side of the roof so that we could see out and have a good view all round. It might be unwise, but the building is high and I can see both artillery gunners, Nathem and Kathem, one on the roof of the Iraqi school down the road and the other on top of the water towers about a mile away near the Bayan Palace. They must have dragged that heavy gun all the way up to the top and they presumably have to walk up and down themselves, or is there a lift? I forgot to mention that about two weeks ago, while the soldiers were bricking in windows and building their pillboxes, they bricked in two of our school windows — I suppose we are lucky they have not knocked out all the glass and bricked everything in. My big fear is that they will use the bricks from the wall round the school and then somehow the whole place will be completely exposed. I wonder if they keep a lot of ammunition in there? If they do, that will undoubtedly mean the school could be precision bombed as well.

10.00 a.m.

We heard very heavy gunfire and explosions shook all the windows and we wondered if this had anything to do with the French mirages that were supposed to have attacked an ammunition dump. Despite the noise going on, the shaking and rattling, quite a number of people came to Friday prayers in the mosque. In a way this mosque and the blue mosque slightly further away are a lifeline for me, for nothing stands in the way of going to prayers. The men from the houses around have been taking it in turns to give the call, but I notice that very few of the soldiers go, though the *Mukhabarat* of course attend to keep an eye on what is going on.

Saturday 19 and Sunday 20 January 1991

I rang my friend Gladys, to see if she was all right and, like me, she has noticed a heavy smell of kerosene, which she had first smelt yesterday. As I normally have little sense of smell, it must have been heavy and I wondered what it came from. All the street lighting is now turned off at night along the beach and in the roads nearby. There is a rumour going around that we are all going to be ordered to reduce the amount of lighting we use at night to a minimum. This is something I do anyway within reason to save on bulbs, which are no longer available. On the other hand, it would not be a good idea to have the house in complete darkness, for then the soldiers would simply try to burgle it. Now that it has become necessary to pay so much more attention to security, most of the doors and windows seem so fragile.

Nadr's cousin, Omar, rang to say that 'black rain' had fallen in their district, so I think that an oil dump or some such thing must have been blown up.

The Free Kuwait Radio in Saudi Arabia has apparently said that no one should open their doors to people dressed in white hospital coats offering to distribute gas masks, for they are actually forcing people to donate blood. The only people I have seen around in white coats, however, work in the Al Hadi Hospital down the road and they are invariably walking wearily back to their homes after long hours on duty.

Soldiers often ask for lifts and since they are usually carrying guns one has little option but to let them in and drop them off as soon as possible. A friend of ours had had to give a lift to two Republican guards who had been at Shuaiber (Iraq), which is 60 kilometres from Basra, and they told him that it had been blown apart yesterday. So that might explain the black rain. My brother-in-law, Abu Fakhry (who lives close to the seafront), said that they had a house inspection yesterday. The soldiers had also looked into the empty houses nearby and had even set fire to a few of them. Being near the sea, Abu Fakhry gets the full blast of the guns on the beach and since everything is shaking and shuddering they tend to spend a good deal of their time in their basement.

My walk today was for 200 yards over to Mr and Mrs Moriwaki's villa opposite one side of the school. Their two sons have been at our school for well over ten years. They are Japanese, but decided to remain behind and thus not to leave Kuwait with the Japanese contingent. Though some of Mr Moriwaki's experiences during that time were unpleasant, he did at least avoid becoming a hostage. They had to move from their former house to where they are now because someone reported them to the authorities. A friend and business partner of theirs is a Kuwaiti fireman who has some pretty hair-raising tales to tell. It must be a great nervous strain for him to have to witness some of the terrible things that he has seen during this period.

The school seems very quiet; they have even removed the artillery gun from the roof. In fact the soldiers do not seem to want it known that there are soldiers there, so I take that to mean there are only normal amounts of ammunition inside. Were it to turn into a dump it would undoubtedly be bombed — a most unpleasant thought. If I look carefully down to the bottom of the road I can see the entrance to the Iranian school, with its Republican guards inside it. They, of course, still have a Kathem manning the large AA gun on top of the building, as there are on top of the water towers a mile away.

Monday 21 January 1991
Absolutely torrential rain. I bet it has been leaking in at the top of the school; it always does. It was dripping in upstairs so Nadr and I ran around with containers of all shapes and sizes to catch it as it came through the joints of the glass at the sides of the roof.

Just before 12.00 p.m. last night the electricity went off in Jabriya. But it was not altogether unexpected or disagreeable and some of the emergency lighting worked quite well. The thought of refrigerators full of food supplies being cut off is, however, more worrying. The lights came back on after a time, first at Ziad's house, then at the house opposite us, where the Abu Huntash family live, and only later at our house and at the mosque. We are obviously all on different electricity phases. As soon as our supply was resumed we turned the TV on to find that more Scuds had been dropped on Damman and Riyadh. There was a fear that they would contain chemical warheads. One of the captured airmen also came onto Baghdad television; he looked as if he had been knocked about, poor man.

This morning the electricity failed again for about ten minutes and then struggled back on once more. There was very heavy firing and clearly some 'big guns' in the distance and this continued off and on throughout the day. Abu Fakhry rang to say that some soldiers had come into his garden, eaten some of the oranges and bitter grapefruit from his trees and then demanded food. For one awful moment I suspect he thought that they might, as they had done in some places, insist on the food being cooked for and served to them. Their food supplies seem to have been disrupted by the bombing and, though they never had that much, they now have nothing at all. They only asked for a little rice and lentils, so he gave them some and they went off to the occupied houses opposite to do their own cooking. If we think that the bread we get is awful, then the bread the army is given is unbelievable. I think the flour must be mixed with wood shavings!

Our immediate area now sounds like a farmyard; there are chickens, some ducks, a few geese (good for burglars) and even guinea fowl, as well as sheep and goats. With all this rain the grass has sprung up and were it a normal year the desert would be beginning to look very beautiful. It reminds me of a weekend we spent at Mutla' Ridge when one of the gullies we went down could have been in Austria or Switzerland. There were flowering bushes, one alive with caterpillars about to turn into chrysalises and another with dozens of little desert bees buzzing around it. In the distance I spotted a desert fox and all the fragile, perfect little desert flowers were waving about in the breeze. The nights were cold and the stars bright and it was delightful to wake before sunrise and drink hot tea. Now even around us the grass is green, but the faces are unhappy and the air rent with the sound of explosions and gunfire.

Tuesday 22 January 1991

I leapt out of bed twice last night for the outbursts of firing were so heavy that I wondered if we ought to go into the basement. All the street lights, at least in Jabriya were off, though not in Rumaithiya. At one point I went to the top of the roof to look out — the two ladders we put there have given us an excellent view in every direction. I looked out towards the Kuwait Towers, slightly round in the direction of Failaka Island (though I could see nothing at all there) and then on around towards the Regency Palace Hotel and finally towards Ahmadi and out to the desert, where I am sure a great deal of the bombing is taking place.

In the afternoons, if it seems safe, I still take my usual short walk, being very careful to keep well away from anyone in uniform. I tend to go down the parallel roads in which many Kuwaitis are still living near the blue mosque, so that if anything happens I can get out of the way.

Riyadh and Dhahran seem to have come under Scud attack again (CNN is now called Scudavision!) but they were brought down by a Patriot missile.

Wednesday 23 January 1991

Scuds landed in Tel Aviv last night and injured many people. How horrible it must be for them being such sitting ducks. I try not to think about the possibility of the same thing happening to us because it seems certain that if it suited the Iraqi regime to toss anything in this direction they would, even if it meant hitting their own soldiers.

Although one of us usually stays in the house when the other is out, this afternoon Nadr and I walked over together to Abu Ali and Rowa to have some tea.

I always try to take sneaky looks down the side roads at the French and Chinese embassies, which are blocked off and surrounded by soldiers living in tents. Anyway I would not dare go too near to them or even stare too hard in their direction. They appear to be incredibly filthy and it is plain that rubbish is never tidied up or burned. Now that I think of it I have never noticed soldiers burning rubbish or throwing anything on the dumps. In school they just toss it out of a window where it lands on the projecting roof with a damp squelch. They all behave like cuckoos fouling their own nests. This could be part of a policy to do as much damage as possible, or it could just be due to the lack of exercise, low morale and failure to keep the army occupied.

As Nadr and I were leaving the house to walk back home, there was a really ferocious outburst of firing. We then heard and indeed saw some planes high above, small specks sailing placidly along with their vapour trails behind them, having presumably dropped their bombs somewhere. Everything and everyone had opened fire on them — obviously Nathem and Kathem from the government school around the corner from us had, and presumably the soldiers in the Chinese and French embassies, on the bridges and in the bricked-in residences had also done so. The house rocked, the windows rattled and the sounds reverberated off the walls. Abu Ali shrieked at us to come back inside and Rowa peered in horror from her window, while walking in measured beat down the road was a man who had now become so used to this that he did not appear to hear it. Although we were all frightened and knew we could get killed, the sense of relief at the Allies having at last begun to force the Iraqis to withdraw enabled us to bear what was now happening.

Rowa and her mother have moved from their flat on the third floor to one on the ground floor and on nights when the bombing is particularly bad they sleep under the table.

We have been told that, as of 12 noon today, there will no longer be any petrol rationing because there is no more petrol, except of course for army vehicles. Things are becoming truly difficult. Kuwait is such a sprawling place and it is difficult to walk far, so how are people going to get to a market to buy food? Not that there is much anyhow. It must be a frightful worry for people with children. Adults can manage on very little, but children cannot.

Thursday 24 January 1991
It has been a cold but sunny day with many bombardments, some of which I actually could not hear. I now leave my bathroom door closed because for some reason it rattles and shakes when something is going on. Today, even when it appeared to be relatively quiet and calm, the door was shaking so much that I thought the piece of coloured glass in the middle of it would fall out.

There were also a series of very deep explosions and I hoped that the oil wells were not being blown up. Our electricity has gone off again, but I have given up being hysterical about it. Mrs Abu Huntash [my neighbour] and I ring each other up constantly and ask, 'What will we do if it goes completely?' We know that we can do nothing but it helps to moan about it. Hers is off at the moment, although Abu Fakhry says theirs is still on in Rumaithiya. He has a small generator and will connect the refrigerator to it as long as he has some petrol from which to run it. Absolutely nothing is happening at our school. Although the army have been shooting from all around us, I suspect that 'our lot' go down into the basement gymnasiums and remain there. I have forgotten who told me, but I believe that a couple of the men ran away not so long ago. [Much later on we found out that this rumour had been true, for it was recorded by the officer in charge that the men had not returned and should be punished when they did. We found the charge book lying in the rubbish at the school.]

Friday 25 January 1991

This morning the clouds were high and puffy and there was some sun, but by midday it had begun to rain again. We think that the Island of Garo [Kuwait] has been recaptured, which would be marvellous. There seems to be a huge black cloud coming from the Shuaiba Port area and Nadr says that last night he saw flames in that direction through his binoculars. The trouble is we see all these things but do not really know exactly what is happening.

The electricity is still somewhat shaky but so far it has kept running. I was listening to the BBC news on the radio when it suddenly cut out and went completely dead. I glanced outside, for I thought it was the electricity once again, but then I wondered if the radio itself had given out. It had after all been on continuously for the past six months and it is quite an old one. I rang Gladys and exactly the same thing had happened to them. Then, after about five or ten minutes, very heavy bombing began and the radio came back on again. It gradually dawned on me that possibly for some reason the Allies had jammed everything and then let fly with the bombs. It was certainly a most severe series of raids.

By noon there was heavy rain, thunder and lightening and, I suppose, bombing as well. It was so dark and cold that it felt like early evening. There was also a 'cloud' that was not a rain one and I wondered if the Iraqis had done something to Sea Island. The rain was not only heavy, but *black* as well and it trickled down the walls and into the yard all black and greasy. When I went down and tried to brush the water away, streaky smudges remained and black lines dripped onto the ground from the palm trees. The rain poured down onto the burned out rubbish heaps and settled in sticky pools on the sand.

8.00 p.m.
I cannot describe our horror at the news that the Iraqis have apparently turned on the taps and oil is spilling out into the Gulf. Everyone rang up everyone else and for once we did not talk too cryptically. This is a crime against all humanity. What on earth should be done about such people? Those responsible for it should be tried as war and environmental criminals.

Saturday 26 January 1991
There was a good deal of shooting and quite a few explosions last night and the bathroom door shook all the time, but I did not even bother to get out of bed. I did get up once during the early-morning prayer and could see that there were quite a number of people in the mosque. Rowa rang and said she had heard that the co-op would open for a short time today, that she would be passing by and she suggested we might also visit the Sultan Centre. So I gave Nadr a cup of tea (very stewed these days, but if anyone complains I tell them about my gypsy friends in England who kept their teapot continuously on the go and though the tea leapt out snarling when it was poured, it tasted pretty good) and told him where I was going. He drank the cup and went off to sleep having been up all night. As might be expected there was even less on the co-op shelves than before. We took our meagre ration of bread, which is now almost dark brown. I am sure it is *good* for us but from being a part-time health nut for brown bread, I never want to see it again. Oh for some crusty white bread with poppy seeds on top! Quite a number of soldiers were wandering around in the co-op, rather despondently though, for all that seemed to be left were bottles of dubious-looking shampoo and a few packets of coconut milk. The co-op's Kuwaiti manager, Abu Hani, was as usual surrounded by a multitude of people arguing and yelling. How he manages to look so calm I do not know.

While Rowa was talking to a friend and I was in an adjoining aisle trying to memorize what little there was on the shelves — had I dared to I would have produced my notebook and written it down — there was a sudden blast of sound. From the nearby government school came shattering staccato bursts of heavy gunfire and a low rumbling sound began to shake the whole building. It was the sort of rumble that begins deep down and works its way to the top. I jumped round, looked up and saw the whole roof shaking backwards and forwards and showers of dust started to float down onto our heads. Women screamed and held their frightened children under their *abat*, men shouted in shocked voices, 'Keep calm. It will be over soon,' and the soldiers, unable to run and hide as they might have preferred to do, tried to appear unconcerned. The three people standing next to me picked up and put down bottles of something with exaggeratedly slow movements and impassive faces. No one actually ran towards the doors; they knew that it was probably worse outside and, as there was nothing to get under, they just shifted nervously around on the floor. The sound of the heavy guns resounded off the walls of the buildings around us and swelled to an ear-splitting stridency; and then it was over. There was dead silence for a second and we all stared around at each other grinning delightedly, even at the soldiers. We were alive and for the moment that was wonderful. Then everyone continued about their business of looking up and down the empty shelves. We had all really just been taking an outing from our houses, for we knew there would be very little to buy even if we had the money.

At home it had been even worse. Nadr was sleeping as usual on the floor in the *diwaniya* when the firing began. It half woke him but he turned over and went back to sleep; after all this was now a part of everyday life. The pounding grew louder and the house began to sway more than usual; he again half rose and again fell back, the whole world grinding and crashing with earthquake monotony. Curiosity finally got the better of him and he got himself up and over to the grille window. As he peered out there was a whooshing, sucking noise and, for the second time, his hair rose on his scalp, he curled into a ball and threw himself into the corner of the room. In Ziad's house every window was blown open and a bird's nest in one of them was completely flattened, its eggs smashed to little bits. Strangely, although a few windows in both houses were cracked and loosened, they did not break; being blown open had probably saved them.

Despite our experience in the co-op Rowa and I still decided to go to the Sultan Centre. We drove past bits of 'dead' cars, round holes in the road and through numerous *tefteesh* (roadblocks), many of which were being manned by mere boys trying to look manly and smoking anything that could pass for a cigarette. Some stern-looking, rather silent men at quite a number of the roadblocks were reputed to be Mauritanians. There are quite a few Somalis around as well; in fact some are living in one of the empty houses opposite us. Nadr and Abu Ali were speaking to them the other day and they mentioned that they came from Somalia. For several years quite a number of Somalis have been working in Iraq as porters. The Iraqis must have employed them to lift and carry when official buildings in Kuwait were being emptied and everything put into trailers for removal to Iraq. The ten or so men living near us go off somewhere every morning and generally return in the late afternoon.

The Sultan Centre looked much emptier than usual and the background noise of distant bombing and gunfire was still continuous. Not many people were out other than a few like ourselves who were hunting for some food or needing a little relief from being inside all the time. We could see that the black rain had made a fearful mess of all the buildings in Kuwait. It had streaked all the walls and tiles like dirty tears and even Saluki [the desert dog] had turned from being a pale champagne colour to a dirty grey. At the best of times Salukis are slender dogs, but he was now emaciated, though we gave him and the cat Fishbone [born at the beginning of the invasion] whatever there was. I doubt if ever in the long history of Salukis there has ever been one the colour he now is. I go into Ziad's house every day and spend a bit of time sitting on the doorstep to try and give the impression that it is occupied. When the planes fly over I can see them high up in the sky and that sets Kathem off and everyone else too. I think the Republicans know perfectly well that the planes are too high up even to hope to touch them, but shooting at them makes them feel better. The sound bouncing off the walls of the house is shattering, but knowing that I am not the one being aimed at means it does not bother me. There is an empty space between two houses across the sand where the men from the houses opposite sit in the weak sun, well wrapped up in their *farwahs* (sheepskin winter coats) staring up at the sky and talking. The children come out as well, but if the noise becomes too ferocious with everything shaking, they get frightened and rush indoors.

The other day I heard that a Kuwaiti had gone onto his roof and had started to take pot shots at the AA gunners, so I am careful to keep myself hidden when I climb out for my regular look around. I have a good view of Kathem from the top of Ziad's house. It must be boring up there as they sit in the AA gun seat twiddling themselves around looking cold and rubbing their hands together. After each firing session he and sometimes his mate get down and 'clean' (?) the gun.

Sunday 27 January 1991

At midnight Nadr tore into the house shouting that huge fires were shooting up out of the desert. I ran to the ladders on the roof as fast as I could and, clinging onto the steel bars, climbed up and looked out towards the desert near the airport [Subhan]. The sky was a glowing red. Immediately there was an explosion, a ball of flame erupted upwards and another flame that pulsated malevolently like a living thing cast a further red and orange glow in the sky. The Iraqis were blowing up Kuwait's oil wells.

That night my feelings of fury and indignation were so intense that I found it impossible to write coherently in my journal. I was too churned up to go back to bed, so I spent the rest of the night up the ladder watching the sky, seeing the black clouds mix with what appeared to be more rain clouds. My journal then notes that Nadr and I felt very depressed at what we had seen. As daylight dawned it was raining heavily. The seagulls were paddling in the black pools of water, their once white feathers now greyer than ever. By mid-morning the rain had eased off somewhat and what sounded like many planes flew over high up, with a few half-hearted shots being aimed at them. The planes had probably dropped their bombs and were idling back to base over Kuwait.

At 5.00 p.m. the planes flew over once more but this time they were so high up that we could only hear the noise of their engines. Tracer sailed into the air with flocks of birds trying to override it; every gun in the vicinity was competing with the call to prayer. People calmly walked round the black puddles to get to the mosque. Some thought that the beaches were being bombed. My friend Hind rang to say that it was bad where they lived. Their shutters had been blown off and she had heard that a missile had slammed into 30 flats in a block in Farwaniya and that someone had lost a leg as a result. Today the Iraqi planes flew up and sneak-landed in Iran, so it seems they do not want to pitch themselves against the Allies.

Monday 28 January 1991

The early-morning sun glowed an angry orange-red. It felt extremely cold and the black cloud stretched round the rim of the sky past Failaka Island. It was quite quiet, though the bathroom door had been rattling. Even the seagulls had not yet arrived to paddle in the murky pools and peck at the rubbish piles — it is very hard to set fire to them with all this rain. I wondered if Kuwait had reached the point at which newspaper reports would say such things as: 'The rubbish is lying around in decaying piles and unless it is cleared soon the population will fall prey to typhoid, cholera and other dreaded diseases.'

Mrs Abu Huntash rang me up to say that the army is after the little battered Suzuki 'because it still has its old KT plates'. Unlike the other cars, which are hidden, being so small and rickety this one had been parked outside pressed against the wall. She denied knowing anything about it and as we were talking on the phone I saw the soldier coming up the road again. Dr Abu Huntash came out and talked to him and managed to send him away. We hurriedly put the Suzuki in the garden of the house two doors down from us where it could not be easily seen from the road.

The electricity went off again for about half an hour. I wondered if the continual bombing and vibrations could be shaking the lines loose. Some people are losing their water as well, but though our pressure is not very good, it manages to trickle in. We are very careful with it. I have remembered how to wash in a 'cupful' of water and use the remains for the indoor plants. Nadr has a more or less good wash now and again.

Tuesday 29 January 1991

There was a clear, starry, moonlit sky last night and from about 1.00 a.m. consistent and regular thumps and thuds could be heard in the distance. Nadr and I went onto the roof, perched ourselves on the ladders and fixed our gaze in the direction of the Ahmadi and Burgan oilfields. On the skyline every few seconds there were gigantic flashes of light, probably from round-the-clock bombing. Anyway I got dressed 'just in case' and, as dawn broke, even went to bed for a short time, still dressed.

The soldier who had been asking about the car has been back again and it seems they are now confiscating cars on no pretext whatsoever. The soldier said that the car was needed as an ambulance, which was so evidently a lie, for one would be hard put to fit an injured person into the Suzuki. They are also arresting people and, we have heard, are killing anyone suspected of having links with the Resistance. It is particularly dangerous for men to be outdoors and very few are now seen on the streets.

Wednesday 30 January, Thursday 31 January 1991
The bathroom door rattled all day and most of last night. The wind dropped in the evening but Kuwait seemed to be covered with an unpleasant haze and a very strong smell of petrol. Mrs Abu Huntash and I talked over the phone and she said that the Al Hamads and Al Khalids had refused to move from their seafront houses. [These are two of Kuwait's most prominent merchant families and many of their members remained in the country during the invasion.] The army wished to throw everybody out and take over the buildings, but they have refused to move even though threatened with death. Because it is so humid tonight (and the humidity often improves TV reception) CNN, Bahrain, Qatar and Saudi are all very clear on the screen. We flick from channel to channel listening to the news and to the commentaries of the various analysts and journalists.

This afternoon Nebila [a neighbour and the Abu Huntashs' daughter] and I decided to take a short walk across the sand and past the Moriwakis' villa. The haze had lifted and, although the smell of petrol still hung in the air, the sky was a cold, clear blue. As we were passing the Moriwakis' villa, the only property overlooked from the side and front of the school, I looked up and saw three planes skimming high up in the sky. At this point every gun in the immediate area let fly, although it must have been quite impossible for any shells to have got even half way near those planes. Gunners on the bridge, in the embassies, on the water towers and, I suppose, along the beaches and everywhere else, fired as hard as they could. I wondered if the whole of Kuwait were trying to hit those planes. Because it sounded so fierce and because we could have been hit by falling shrapnel, we sheltered under a small shop overhang and I was able to see straight down the road to the front of the school. I nudged Nebila and pointed to about 15 men, not in uniform but in dark winter *dishdashas*, tottering out from the front gate under the trees, staring up at the sky and quickly retreating out of sight. It looked as if they had not wanted to be seen. That particular raid lasted for about 20 minutes and afterwards we walked slowly home.

Abu Ali and others say that *tefteesh* [roadblocks] have become more widespread and unpleasant than ever. Everyone, in and out of uniform, is taking part in them — soldiers, police, *Mubahath* [intelligence] and even some of the Palestinian groups that presumably came in with the Iraqis. They are all as sour, rude and disagreeable as it is possible to be. They make drivers and passengers get out of their vehicles, they open the boots of their cars and they arrest whomever they want on the flimsiest of pretexts. It seems quite possible that there will be more house searches. I have heard that the Resistance has been active again. I saw a group of dangerous-looking, heavily armed T-shirted young men near to the once-thriving pre-school nursery by the Al Hadi Hospital. They were climbing out of two large trucks and swaggering into some flats holding their AK47 rifles at the ready. They looked trained and as if they knew how to use their guns, so I suspect they might well belong to a group like Abu Nidal. A few days later when I went past again they had disappeared.

Friday 1 February 1991 (six months too long)

The soldiers in the school were on top of the roof, having knocked down one of the water tanks, and were once again setting up a gun emplacement. It does not appear to be like the one Kathem has, but it is impossible to see it clearly. Bombing continued throughout the day and Omar [Nadr's cousin] said that in their district [Kaifan] they were being showered with bits from a ship (or ships) that had been blown up in the port.

A soldier, apparently from the school, had phoned Abu Fakhry and, speaking quickly and nervously, had said that the school buses were going to be taken away and that Abu Fakhry ought to come in to prevent it from happening. The man rang twice, the second time to say that they were being removed at that moment. I rushed up to the roof, but unfortunately could not see that side of the school. Abu Fakhry dared not go over, for men were being taken away for no reason at all and he could well have found himself a prisoner along with the buses. Even the boys, who until fairly recently played a little football near the mosque, stay indoors now. If they do come out they keep near their front doors ready to dart back inside if necessary.

There is no lighting on the Fifth Ring Road and our street lights have gone out, but since there seem to be some on near the blue mosque, I presume that the vibrations from the bombing have knocked out some of the lines.

Saturday 2 February 1991

When I went up on the roof early this morning for my daily look at the Kuwait Towers (the symbol of modern Kuwait still standing pointing up to the sky) I noticed a black column of smoke not far behind them. This came from a new type of explosion which erupts in the air leaving behind puffs of smoke that float along somewhat like soap bubbles; the seagulls seem to find them amusing and glide around in concert with them.

Nadr and I went out to try and buy some cigarettes, which are now like gold dust. A pack of 20, if it can be found, can fetch anything from between ID 2 and ID 300, though a pack of 30 small Bidis (small, stale, dried-up herbal-type Indian smokes) can be found for as little as ID 1. On the way to the *baqala* [small local grocery] I looked up at the gunner on the water tank towers and could see his gun but not him. I know from watching from the top of the roof that when he is not twirling his gun round and round, he is lying flat out on a stolen sun chair, very often with his back to the shooting. As a professional he is aware that it is usually a waste of time to engage in frantic bursts of gunfire when the planes are over 30,000 feet up.

Bombing went on for quite some time and the planes could be heard high up. Occasionally vapour trails criss-crossed the sky and I tried to photograph them. One could hear mighty thuds as the ground was being hit in the Maseela beach area, inland towards Mishrif and along the seafront there. It was maddening to hear all this, feel it, even smell it, but not to know exactly what was happening. There was quite a strong smell of cordite in the air. Then Nadr came out with a pair of binoculars and said that the aeroplanes were B52s, which, it transpired, they were.

The water pressure is very low now and the electricity comes and goes. Soon I know it will go and I will get my wish to see the stars in the sky as they used to be in the 'old' days. The trouble is it would not be under the same circumstances at all and I would therefore prefer to forgo that pleasure.

The area near and around the Dutch Embassy is crawling with army personnel. They have really dug themselves in, so that is yet another place where no one can walk.

Sunday 3 February 1991
The weather was cloudy, still and (alarmingly) rather stuffy. I wondered what I would do about all the textiles upstairs when the electricity finally went off. Nothing much can be done and, anyhow, the whole place might be burned down, especially if it comes to street fighting. It would be sad if they were destroyed, for museum artefacts are usually records of a nicer side of human endeavour.

While some heavy bombing was going on a little boy from down the road was outside with a toy gun going 't---t---tat---'. I wondered if he was frightened and whom he imagined he was shooting.

CNN came through quite well in the evening, but had to compete with a particularly violent barrage of firing. We were not sure what the targets of all this activity were, but thought they might be on the beaches. Nathem and Kathem joined in with considerable vigour. I notice that their return fire is becoming less frequent, the bombing more so (it seems to continue all day and most of the night now) and I heard on the radio that, as of 2 February, there had been 37,000 Allied air sorties. Everything sways and shakes and it is fortunate that most of the buildings in Kuwait are so strongly constructed, otherwise they would have been shaken to bits long ago.

A breeze came up in the evening, along with an odd haze, which might have been light sand mixed with something else. We all wondered if there were any chemicals or biological germs in it, for it did smell a little, but the chickens did not die and the Saluki, now a dark grey apparition with his ribs protruding more than ever, skipped around as energetically as always.

Monday 4 February 1991

The director's house was broken into again and Abu Ali went over to try and make it more secure by putting cut-off broomsticks along the windows so that they would be more difficult to push open.

The school buses have practically all gone. Abu Fakhry said that he drove up and down the main expressway trying to catch a glimpse of what remained of them. A few were still there, but they were without their wheels and engines and most of their windows had been kicked in. I suppose we shall never know exactly who took the others and where they went.

It was a fairly quiet day from the bombing point of view, but the bathroom door continued to shake and rattle so the Allies must be working out in the desert.

It was announced that only military personnel in Iraq were allowed petrol — 'Fuel supplies to the public are being halted due to the damage to installations.'

It is too dangerous to use cars now and no one would dream of driving in a clean shiny one. The older and more battered they are the better, but even that does not prevent them from being taken. So anyone who has a bicycle is now riding one. We have a rather rickety one that Mr Khan left behind and one that I had used for riding along the footpath. Abu Ali has found one as well.

Tuesday 5 February 1991

A young Kuwaiti aged 20 has just been shot dead in front of his house. The *Mukhabarat* came to his front door, asked him his name, if his father had been in the army and if he were now in prison. To the reply, 'Yes', they shot him there and then and left his body lying on the doorstep.

Wednesday 6 February 1991

There have been heavy bombing raids, with many thuds and explosions. Some that are further away can be felt through one's feet, but not necessarily heard; with others the doors and windows rattle and shake; for the rest columns of black smoke rise in the air. The smoke from the burning rubbish tips tends to be greyer and more feathery and, of course, fades into the atmosphere more quickly.

Both CNN and Dubai TV showed clips of Kuwaiti interpreters getting ready to come and help in Saudi Arabia. We recognized Ziad amongst them, which was very exciting. He was one of 40 Kuwaiti interpreters and we had caught two brief glimpses of him before on television.

Thursday 7 February 1991
Our phone is now dead and I know that other districts have lost their lines as well. The electricity cuts out every day now, but so far has continued to come back on.

A strange and rather nerve-wracking thing happened early this evening. We were listening to the radio and drinking our stewed tea when we became aware that someone was pounding on the outside door. We looked out and saw Abu G, the Iraqi Embassy parent who had helped get Nadr and Abu Ali released after their arrest. We rarely saw him and indeed did not even know that he was still in Kuwait. Reluctantly Nadr went down to let him in, wondering if he brought bad news, good news or any news at all — he was surely not coming merely to pass the time of day. I quickly pushed the radio out of sight and looked around to see if anything else should be concealed. There were numerous books on Islamic art, textiles and language, as well as a few cookery ones. I removed the fax machine which had been placed under the shelf. Abu G came upstairs and into the kitchen and sat down at the table, his eyes darting around and taking everything in.

Nadr sat facing him across the table; I sat next to the window with the bookshelf just behind me now covered with a cloth down its length to save the books from the pollution in the air. Abu G suddenly got up and walked to the stove behind us and stood staring over in the direction of the cupboards. Our eyes followed him and we looked in the direction of his gaze, but saw nothing of any conceivable interest. I wondered if he could see something that we could not. His cold eyes passed over in my direction and he returned to his seat. I poured tea for us all and sat down beside him.

He remarked that he was now in the army out in Jahra and we both chorused, '*the army?*' — we knew that he had to be in the *Mukhabarat*, for we did not see him in a mere barracks. He said everyone was in the army now. We made no comment but were not quite sure what that might mean. To make conversation Nadr asked

166

him what it was like out in Jahra, for we knew that out in that direction there had been bombing day and night, which he coolly confirmed. I asked how his wife and child were and whether they were in Baghdad. They were outside in a small town somewhere away from the bombing.

While we were wondering why he had come, he suddenly asked Nadr if he had any computers or electronics, for he had heard that Nadr was an electronic engineer. I stared down into my teacup and stirred the already mixed sugar, and Nadr calmly replied, 'Yes, he was and yes he did.'

'Show me them then, where do you keep them?'

'I will take you to see them', he answered.

Abu G slowly drank his tea, his eyes still looking at everything in the kitchen. His head swivelled to the cloth covering the bookshelf next to me and to my horror I remembered we had received a FREE KUWAIT badge in the last box from Jordan and that I had defiantly pinned it onto the cloth half way up. Abu G was staring over my head directly at it. He read out slowly and deliberately 'Fee Reee KU...wa...it'. He repeated the words and then looked unsmilingly at me. I stared back at him and there seemed to be little to say. He gave a small humourless grimace and I continued to gaze at him until Nadr said, in the somewhat pregnant silence, 'Would you like to come and see my computers?'

Abu G got up and they went upstairs together. Later on, but not until Abu G had gone, I unpinned the FREE KUWAIT badge and placed it instead on the inside of the cloth.

Nadr did not show Abu G the hidden space behind the main room where all his computers were. In what was normally an exhibition area there were a few computers, monitors and keyboards that had been rescued from the school lying on the floor along with some nineteenth-century Arab paintings that had been removed from elsewhere.

Abu G looked at these, glanced at the paintings and other odds and ends, turned to Nadr and remarked, 'Hide these. There are going to be more house searches soon. Put them and any photographs and suchlike out of the way.' With that he turned on his heel and came downstairs again. He remained a short while saying he had to get back to Jahra and we never saw him again.

Friday 8 February 1991

Last night the sky was such a spectacular sight that we assumed an ammunition dump had been blown up. It was like a gigantic fireworks display. There were flashes and explosions, with haloes of sparks, one following another, and the already red and orange sky becoming a deep throbbing red. We spent a long time watching it and wondering just what had happened.

The phones have now gone completely dead so we cannot ring anyone and the electricity cuts are more frequent and for longer periods. The water pressure is very low and such water as there is is used for multiple purposes. The planes flew over as usual, with bombs dropping and all the doors and windows shaking — in fact I sometimes think that the bathroom door will fall off its hinges. There is much less shooting now from the army. I hope and believe it is becoming really frightened by this awesome display of technological power.

Nadr has put all the computers into the air-conditioning ducts, as well as anything else that might attract attention if there are to be more house searches. We spent a long time collecting all these things together. Nadr had to unscrew all the grilles over the ducts, we then wrapped as much as we could in plastic and he pushed it all back as far as possible.

Saturday 9 February 1991

It was a cool, sunny, breezy morning and the 'black' clouds lying on the horizon were the only ones in the sky.

Last night there was yet another Scud attack on Israel with about 20 people injured and widespread damage.

We listened to a discussion about the problems of the Lithuanians on the radio in which it was felt that too many people had been killed for such a small country. The same goes for Kuwait, which is also a small country and cannot afford to lose its people. We thought of the 10,000 Kuwaiti POWs in prisons all over Iraq and wondered what Kuwait had done to deserve all this.

This afternoon Rowa, Umm Ali and I decided to walk past the hospital, under the bridge and into Hawalli to yet another street market. We needed to see if we could buy potatoes, tomatoes and eggs, for these were still arriving by lorry from Jordan. We walked along several nearly empty streets (skirting the government schools in which the army were barracked), under the bridge and into a wide street where the vendors sat with their so-called goods spread out on orange boxes or suitcases. Tinned milk was non-existent and there was no flour, sugar, oil or rice — in fact there were no basics. Bottles of shampoo were available and, strangely, an occasional tin of cocoa or drinking chocolate, as well as packets of soap powder, which were all useless at the moment because water was in such short supply.

We paused longingly in front of an orange box on which a solitary bar of Toblerone chocolate lay in the sun. We walked on, looked at each other, then went back and admired it once more. The bar was the smallest of the Toblerone range, but could have been divided into three delicious pieces. It cost ID 10, was half melted and old as well. Umm Ali tried to bargain with the salesman but he was not interested and even Rowa could not get him to lower the price a little. So guiltily the money and the chocolate changed hands and we ate it there and then. It was perfectly horrible, with white patches on it from having lain in the sun for too long, but we enjoyed every mouthful. For a brief moment our spirits lifted and we carried on looking at onions, tomatoes and potatoes.

A few of the once-flourishing groceries were open, but their stocks were very low, although, being shopkeepers, they had tried forlornly to give the impression of plenty by putting bottles of this and that along the fronts of their shelves. Rowa picked up some pitted tomatoes and sprouting onions and asked the young man serving if he had anything better.

'No', he replied slowly, 'That is from the last lorry load that will come through from Jordan.'

'No more will come?' she asked.

'No, the lorries are being blasted off the road now and so nothing can come through. Anyhow what does it matter? We are all going to die in a few days from germ warfare, we'll all be dead soon.'

For some reason, slightly hysterically, we found that very funny and everyone in the shop began laughing and making dark jokes about our imminent deaths, the young man included. It seemed strange that we could contemplate death with such grim humour. Rowa bought a few of the pitted tomatoes and, still grinning, we left the shop.

169

We knew that the Jordan–Iraq route was being heavily bombed as not only vegetables travelled along it, but, by all accounts, other more dangerous objects as well.

Sunday 10 February 1991
There is a *huge* black cloud on the skyline behind the Kuwait Towers. The usual ground-shaking thuds and thumps are continuing all the time. On TV and radio the Iraqis have been moaning about the Allies being war criminals and tyrannical. In short, they have been accusing them of being everything that they themselves are.

Monday 11 February 1991
The pall of heavy smoke that started behind the Kuwait Towers is now hanging over Salmiya and Rumaithiya and is slowly moving over in our direction as well.

We all queued for bottles of gas outside the co-op and stood there for some hours. 'It's coming in now.' 'No, it isn't.' 'Only another half hour.' The long snake-like queue shifted and curled into the road, with occasional arguments and quarrels breaking out. In the end no gas came and it seemed that there was little hope of anyone finding any anywhere.

Everyone rides bicycles now, or else walks; there are hardly any cars on the roads, only military vehicles.

Tuesday 12 February 1991
More Scuds fell in both Israel and Riyadh last night.

No phones, no petrol, no cooking gas, little food and the electricity cannot possibly last for much longer. The water pressure is very low — in fact there is hardly any at all.

Kathem and Nathem now rarely bother even to look at the planes or listen to the explosions. I was watching Nathem through our binoculars and he was sitting on a deck chair by his gun relaxing with his arms behind his head. The main bombing was going on behind him and he ignored it completely.

About 50 oil fires are now raging in the oilfields, all of which have been started by the Iraqis and not by the bombing.

Liberation

Wednesday 13 February 1991

There is no water coming through at all, not even a trickle and it is the same for everyone. We tried to get what water there was left in Ziad's tank over to our house via a pipe between the two buildings. In the middle of doing that, while we were perched on the top of the roof, at least seven planes appeared directly overhead. Kathem went into a veritable orgy of firing, so we had to stop for a while in case any shrapnel came down and hit us. Everyone else is also on top of their roofs struggling with tanks and trying to do something about their diminishing water supplies.

While I was walking over to see how the Moriwakis were, I saw some Tornadoes high up in the sky, rolling and turning and criss-crossing each other's vapour clouds. They must have released their bombs, maybe along the coastline somewhere. Everyone came out to look at them, including the soldiers from the Iranian school. Kathem was inspired and, for about ten minutes, shot vainly in their direction, setting Nathem off as well.

It has been reported on the television that some 450 people have been killed in a bomb shelter in Baghdad and no doubt there will be a great outcry from peace activists and journalists. They ought to come here and see what is happening in Kuwait: they should see how many Kuwaitis are being tortured and imprisoned, both here and throughout Iraq.

Thursday 14 February 1991

All the news has been about the people killed in the Baghdad bunker. Naturally the Iraqi authorities are making as much propaganda capital out of it as they can. My instinct tells me that the victims were probably innocent civilians, but that the bunker had been used by the Iraqis for purposes other than as a shelter. There has been a rumour circulating around here, however, that the people in the bunker may actually have been Kuwaitis or other political prisoners from an Iraqi gaol. People are expendable to the regime and it angers me to think that the Iraqis are at liberty to murder as and when and how they wish, while the Allies have to be 'civilized'.

I cannot help but suspect that the weeping of the relatives standing outside in crowds is a theatrical show. It is too restrained and controlled for a true Iraqi occasion of that type. Funerals there are generally far more tumultuous, with much tearing of hair and ripping of clothes and hysterics. It somehow reminds me of the propaganda films that were made in Kuwait at the beginning of the occupation, when people were rounded up and forced to put on a display of emotion. In any case I have become so cynical about Iraqis now that even if they told me that 'grass was green', I would check on it first before believing a word they said.

Bombing went on for most of the day, with bursts of counter-shooting, especially when the B52s went over. They were high up, so it must have been a waste of ammunition.

Friday 15 February 1991
The door rattled and the barrage was clearly audible all night. I got up early and looked out of all the windows to see if there was an army presence, which could mean the possibility of house searches. Then I went down into the garden to collect the drips from the pump in a bucket, for I wanted to try and water the garden.

3.15 p.m.
We had been up on the roof again, Nadr as usual trying to mend pumps while I watched the military traffic on the road and kept a cautious eye on Kathem, for he was quite likely to take a shot at anyone on a roof.

There were no planes in the sky for a while, just a calm silence. Then pandemonium broke out. Nathem, Kathem, AA guns, shot guns, heavy guns, pistols and anything else that could shoot resounded around the sky; flares winged their way upwards and there may even have been a sound of distant cheering. As I peered further over the wall, Nadr rushed off to grab a radio and twiddle its knobs. Were we about to be killed or had the war ended? Kathem was spinning round in his chair shooting frantically and I ducked because so much was blasting into the sky and falling back to the ground that death by shrapnel pieces was a strong possibility.

From Baghdad Nadr caught the last words of a sensational announcement that Iraq was about to withdraw from Kuwait. We rushed downstairs and turned on CNN. It was indistinct, but sounded like a withdrawal. Outside it seemed as if every bit of ammunition in Kuwait was going up in the air, but the euphoria was short-lived.

There was to be no withdrawal without an array of unacceptable conditions and yet more delaying tactics. The list of what the Allies had to do was quite absurd and even those most keen to end the war could not go along with its stipulations, one of which was 'a guarantee that Kuwait's political system be based on the will of the people and nationalist and Islamic forces and not on the will of the ruling Al Sabah family'. Of most immediate concern to the people of Kuwait was the removal of Iraq from their territory.

Saturday 16 February 1991
At midnight last night the electricity went off all over Kuwait, so my wish to see the stars was granted. Unfortunately the experience was somewhat marred by heavy black clouds, some kind of 'mist' and a very strong smell in the atmosphere. Mrs Abu Huntash asked a young man on a bicycle if he knew anything about the electricity and he said that the vibrations from the bombing had probably caused the lines to come down and crack.

During the day the sun disappeared behind the clouds, there was no water and absolutely everybody felt depressed. The electricity came on late in the evening, flickering somewhat, but before it did, Nadr and I had decided to have a barbecue on top of the kitchen table with the last of some meat from the refrigerator; it was quite fun.

Later in the night Nadr watched some planes flying lazily over and around with their strobe lights on. Not a single shot was fired at them — they just roamed about as they pleased. There was very heavy bombing all night.

Sunday 17 February 1991
The weather has turned very nasty again, with black rain falling everywhere. The yard is awash with this iridescent, shimmering greasy water, the grass is no longer green and the 'ethel' (tamarisk) trees have turned dark and dramatic. The black is coming into the house, on the floor and everything and everybody seems dirty. As for the water, Nadr has been spending most of his time trying to do something about the pumps and tanks at our house, as well as at Abu Ali's and Rowa's. At 6.00 p.m. the water came on and I placed myself under the tap in the garden and had a quick attempt at a cold wash.

There was a very big roadblock at the end of the road opposite the three schools and for about three or four hours any cars that still happened to be around were minutely inspected. Their boots were opened, the underneaths of their engines were examined and some of them were confiscated. Now that telephone links have gone, no one really knows what is happening other than in their immediate area.

Monday 18 February 1991

The early-morning call to prayer alternated with bombs falling. Strangely these particular ones did not cause the doors to rattle, which I do not understand. The bombs just fell.

The Iraqis (here my language is unrepeatable) do not appear to be moving out at all. On the contrary, judging from the amount of traffic on the Fifth Ring Road, they are moving *in*. They must be anticipating a seaborne invasion and want to take advantage of the protection of a residential area.

CNN came on quite clearly and we were just in time to see an Apache helicopter out in the desert herding a group of surrendering soldiers towards a suitable post. It was quite funny.

While Nadr was mending a pump up on Abu Ali's roof he stood up and hit his head hard on a part of the air conditioning. He has quite a bump on his head and eventually had to come home and go to sleep. Under normal circumstances he would probably have gone to a clinic and got some treatment. However, whatever happens now one has to do the best one can with whatever there is at hand.

Rowa, Muna, Taghrid and I went out for a walk in search of cigarettes of any kind. The few that are left are an incredible price, which rises all the time. Although the whole area is greasy and dirty the grass still continues to grow, with the new bits showing brilliant green above the black.

Tuesday 19 February 1991

I forgot to mention three nights ago that the back of the Bayan Palace complex seemed to be on fire. We watched it for ages and thought the Iraqis had almost certainly set it alight. Some fire engines appeared; we could hear their sirens wailing, but long after the fire (if that is what it was) had started. From what little we can see, the area seems to be all blackened and burned out.

174

There is a rumour being passed round that more Kuwaitis are being picked up and taken off to prison and that some of them are being executed. A man in a car suddenly pulled up next to Nadr and Nebil [our neighbour] to tell them that men, or even boys, should be very careful not to be seen outdoors, in fact it would be better still to hide. He got back into his car and hurried off to warn as many other people as he could.

Iraq's foreign minister, Tareq Aziz, is back from his visit to Moscow, but is expected to return for more talks. We are all petrified, for we know they are playing for time because they want to implement a scorched earth policy in Kuwait. And we know that if they are given more time we will all surely die.

According to rumour again, it seems possible that chemical weapons might be used against the population. [There was later some confirmation of this in documents recovered, bombs found with 'Danger–Chemical' written on them and a drawing indicating sites for destruction by chemicals.]

Wednesday 20 February 1991
It rained heavily for most of the day and the roofs leaked once more, so Nadr tried to clean the dust from the sides. I mopped up and used the water on our now rather bedraggled house plants.

6.00 p.m.
We were sitting as usual by the window when Nadr looked up and glanced outside. There seemed to be dozens of armed Red Beret soldiers milling around just below us. Nadr said, 'Damn, it must be *tefteesh*.' I leapt up to check that nothing electrical, no radios etc., were anywhere to be seen and that as little as possible was on view. Dust sheets covered the books on the chests, partly to prevent the black dust settling on them, but also to conceal them from prying eyes.

I wanted to go down and open the door instead of Nadr and we had a short, fierce argument about it, but he absolutely insisted on doing it. There was little time to debate the matter, for they would kick the door in if it were not opened instantly. I remained watching out of the window. A large red wanette, which had undoubtedly been stolen, drove onto the sand and stopped near the edge of the road, with more soldiers piling out and running across to line up down the side of the

Abu Huntash house opposite and in front of our house. They stood with their guns at the ready. The machine gun mounted on the roof of the pick-up swivelled round and pointed directly towards our house. It was at that moment, as army jeeps drew to a stop down below and I saw more men heading for our front door, that I realized it was not an area search at all. We were the objects of interest: the army with its guns had for some reason come for us.

I dragged open the kitchen door and began to run downstairs. I could hear voices at the entrance talking crossly and loudly and then the sound of footsteps approaching, so I backed up again, for they were coming towards the kitchen. What were undoubtedly two members of the *Mukhabarat*, with Nadr just in front and followed by soldiers, marched through the door and straight into the kitchen. The two *Mukhabarat* men nodded coldly in my direction and, for a second or so, everything went quite blank and I could remember nothing. A couple of the soldiers behind them had stepped into the sitting area and switched on the lights. One soldier plonked himself down on the sofa, his rifle butt on the seat, and sat staring at the now rather ragged indoor garden. It had been watered, but only just, for keeping things looking attractive was low on our list of priorities right now and anyhow water was in short supply. A couple of others roamed around poking into cupboards, with the main bulk of men either clogging up the entrance or half way up the stairs.

Another tubby cold-eyed *Mukhabarat* man glanced about angrily and snapped at Nadr, 'I don't want to come here, I want to go downstairs.' He jabbed with his finger downwards and pushed at Nadr with his other hand. Both of us understood down to mean to the flat below.

Everyone began to pile out onto the stairs and I followed behind. The *Mukhabarat* man turned and snapped, 'Stay there in the kitchen,' and a soldier, pointing his rifle towards my stomach, blocked my path. There was nothing I could do but remain and resentfully I went and stood by the window. I could see them all moving outside.

Then a few moments later I saw Nadr, his face strained, being manhandled along the path. The guard had withdrawn from the kitchen and I tore downstairs to the bottom to find some eight or ten soldiers standing around the doorway with guns, which they pointed at me when I tried to follow the main group.

Later I found out that Nadr had taken them, as he thought they required, into the flat below where, in passing, they arrested two visiting men who were peacefully drinking tea and chatting. The men were manhandled off into a jeep and it took their relatives six hours to secure their release, though they had done nothing — they were even beaten for their pains. The relatives probably had to pay a large sum of money to get them back.

I stood at the bottom of the steps waiting for an opportunity to go wherever Nadr was being taken, which I suspected was the museum in the basement. I contented myself by glaring at the soldiers, especially the nearest one, a young man who shifted uncomfortably from foot to foot, his rifle jingling slightly.

Nadr had been ordered to open the main door of the museum and they all went inside and down the steps lined with cheap pieces of brass to give the impression that *this* was the museum. The bottom entrance was blocked, with the two large display cases on either side still shining with their objects and labels inside. I knew that the main door had been opened because a soldier came up and whispered to another, 'It's a museum.' Presumably they had not known exactly what was happening.

In the middle of all this the call to prayer was given and the bombing continued loudly in the background. Both the *Mukhabarat* men, of whom there was a 'nice' one and a 'nasty' one, stared at the swords and knives in one of the cases, turned round and ordered Nadr to take them into the basement — so that was what they had wanted.

'Oh yes', said Nadr and, as arranged, he leapt up the steps to lead them to the other empty and packed-away side of the museum. No one moved. The *Mukhabarat* man swivelled his eyes, pointed his finger straight at the large nineteenth-century Egyptian cupboard blocking the entrance to the museum proper and said, 'In there, I want to go there. Open it up.' Nadr, already half way up the steps, returned down trying to look surprised and muttered, 'Er, yes, oh yes, I forgot.'

The soldiers moved the heavy cupboard and, with a pickaxe, tore the wood from the front. They then tried to smash in the heavy, carved, decorated door underneath. Nadr stopped them and said there was a key and the padlock could easily be opened. He came up to where I was standing on the steps to get it. Outside, through the door by the jeep, our bad-tempered cat Dali was lying on the warm engine purring

177

and being stroked by an officer. Somewhat to my alarm I saw the man turn him over, tickle his ears and pull his tail. Dali hates his tail even being stroked, I held my breath and waited for Dali possibly to put his life in jeopardy by striking out with his claws. Nothing happened and the officer continued to pat him. The waif Fishbone, still a scrawny little black kitten, rubbed his chin on a somewhat embarrassed soldier's boot, the bombing shook everything and prayers could be heard from the mosque. I said mine as well and followed Nadr down the museum steps, expecting to be stopped. I was allowed off the steps but not into the actual museum.

Inside Nadr was questioned and occasionally cuffed and poked with a gun, by first the nice and then the nasty *Mukhabarat* man.

'Where is your father? Where is your brother? Do they live in America now?'

'No, they are in Jordan. No, not in America.'

The nasty interrogator suddenly remarked.

'You know, we know everything about you, everything. We know you. We know all about the silver presents [?] you have received, everything and [triumphantly] we know your name is *Ziad*, your name is Ziad, isn't it? It's Ziad [pause].'

'No, it's Nadr,' replied Nadr flatly.

This silenced the men for the time being and, ordering Nadr to stay where he was, they began to walk round glancing at the exhibits. They did not appear to be aware that there was a blocked-off empty side and an inner room filled with gold jewellery and small items of antique furniture. Neither did they realize that, packed away behind the false wall, there were some silver horses.

When everything was being hastily removed and hidden, we had totally overlooked an eighteenth-century gold and enamel Mughal necklace. It was a good example of the exceedingly fine enamel work of that period and this particular item had probably been made in Jaipur. It had lain ignored and forgotten in its glass case, until Nadr was called over by the two *Mukhabarat* men.

Pointing towards it one said, 'Is that thing made of gold?'

Polite surprise written on his face, Nadr answered, 'No of course not, it's brass.'

Whether or not they believed him we will never know, but they nodded slightly and went back to business.

Looking up at the ceiling of false slats overhead, the one said menacingly, 'We know that you have been harbouring ammunition up there, you have haven't you?'

'No, there is nothing up there, just pipes.'

'There are arms there. Do not lie. We will send someone up and then you will be in real trouble.'

'Send somebody up,' said Nadr. 'There's nothing there as I just said.' A soldier was despatched to inspect the area above the false ceiling and, although we could well have done with a cache of arms, there was nothing there. While packing away we had briefly considered the area, but had rejected it on the grounds that it was too obvious a hiding place.

They came to a stop in front of a small, fragile office door and ordered Nadr to open it. He came out again and asked if I knew where the key was and, thinking it was in one of the drawers, I began to scrabble around for it. I was sure I could find it. While I was doing this the nice *Mukhabarat* man came out towards me and, with a false smile pinned to his face, murmured smoothly.

'*Laat Khafee Hajjia, Laat Khafee.*' [Do not be frightened *Hajjia* — *Hajjia* is an honorific title for an older woman.]

Still shifting papers in the drawer and mumbling something meaningless, I replied, 'I do not know where the key is, please push the door open, it does not matter.'

'Oh no,' he replied, '*We* do not want to do that.'

A ridiculous interlude followed with me insisting he break or push the door open and him refusing to do so. We both knew what he would prefer to do and, for that matter, I knew what I would have liked to do — if only I had the means. These polite exchanges continued for about a minute before he 'reluctantly' turned to go back to the office door.

Back inside, with his false smile wiped off his face, the door, which could easily have been pushed in, was axed down by the army (with the help of their boots) into almost matchstick-size pieces. Inside the small office, which is furnished with a table and chair and has its display cases (which contain a variety of Arab swords and daggers) flat against the wall, are a couple of antique guns with long decorative barrels. Both the *Mukhabarat* men stared inside thoughtfully and one, turning to Nadr, enquired, 'Do these things still work?'

Rather unwisely Nadr answered, 'Of course — 300 years ago,' for which he received another slap around the jaw.

After well over an hour down in the museum they slowly began to move upstairs and that was when the real anxiety began. Would they take Nadr off with them? They were acting as if that might well happen. I hovered as close behind as I dared, though not at all sure what I would do if he were suddenly hustled into a jeep. The two other unfortunate men had been removed and, for a moment, it looked as if Nadr was once again going to find himself back in a police station. Then, suddenly, the men from the *Mukhabarat* and the soldiers with their rifles swung up into their vehicles and, with a revving of engines and a certain amount of dark menace, they and the wanette filled with men and a machine gun moved off down the road.

The strangest thing was that our neighbours opposite, who had been watching the news on their television, had seen and heard nothing, but then I suppose the sounds of bombing did not help. We tottered upstairs, relieved at the outcome, although our one remaining guard had lost his precious (and expensive) carton of cigarettes and some odds and ends had been pilfered from the small office. We know they will be back; we feel it in our bones. This is not the end of the matter, but perhaps something will happen before they get back.

Thursday 21 February 1991
Cars and other vehicles (especially if they still have their original numberplates) are being stolen from everywhere and with no pretences or excuses now — people are just told, 'Get out of the car.' Soldiers are walking or driving around peering through gates, into garages, anywhere and everywhere, and taking what they will. The little Suzuki cannot be easily seen from the road and the cars down the sides of Ziad's house barely show from the road and are, in any case, covered up. Once more someone came by, at considerable danger to himself, to tell everyone to keep indoors. He warned that even women were in danger, but especially boys and men, and that they should not even stand on their doorsteps. They are picking up men and pushing them into buses and taking them away.

The army has broken into a friend's house and removed the father. The teenage daughter locked herself into the bathroom and the younger children hid in the garden. [The father was returned to Kuwait

three weeks later, after having spent time in various prisons in Iraq.]
Just down the road from us relatives saw a lorry draw up beside two
teenage boys out on their bicycles — they too were taken away.

Friday 22 February 1991
It was Nadr's 29th birthday today and Rowa made him a small cake
and we sang a rather glum 'Happy Birthday'.

We have heard that most of Basra's population has retreated from
the town because of the bombing.

At around midnight Nadr called me up onto the roof to see yet more
oil wells burning in the direction of Ahmadi. We can hear for
ourselves that the Iraqis have been setting off more of the dynamite
placed around the well heads because the explosions go upwards. The
dynamite was set weeks ago. I remember Nebila Abu Huntash telling
us about it and about how they had tried to disconnect some of the
wires, but that the Iraqis had found out and reconnected them.

The sky is a throbbing, burning red. Some of the flames rise and fall
steadily, others shoot straight up in the air to a great height and, I
imagine, let out a mighty roar of theatrical proportions. Yet others are
almost palpably alive: they spurt out in a swollen ball that pulsates
steadily with evil intensity. By comparison, the one accidental oil
blowout in the desert in the 1960s seems like a mere pinprick. At that
time anyone with any transport from Ahmadi and Kuwait town had
rushed out every evening to look at the flare shooting up into the air.
So many people came out that the police had to keep us all from
trying to stand too close. It was said that snakes had also been
attracted by the heat and had turned up from all over the desert. The
blowout had been an awesome display of nature's unleashed power
and was accepted as such. What is happening now is a monstrous
crime against humanity perpetrated by the Iraqi regime and the
engineers who agreed to such a thing. The entire sky this morning was
black. It blotted out the sun and ruined what should otherwise have
been a balmy spring day.

We could not believe that the Russians had asked for a couple more
days for further talks. Can it be possible that they do not understand
what will happen to everyone in Kuwait? We know, we absolutely
know, that what the Iraqis plan if they have to withdraw is to murder
every living soul and smash everything they can lay their hands on.

They will need time if they intend to flatten the buildings because, for the most part, they are built of very solid cement and would be difficult to level. I suppose that is partly why so many buildings have withstood the blasts. [At this point my journal contains some fairly abusive remarks.]

My brother-in-law, Abu Fakhry, narrowly escaped being arrested in the Amman Street souk. He and Abu Yaseen had been trying to buy some eggs (there were none) when a bus and an assortment of cars drew up in the vicinity. What must have been a plainclothes man came up and demanded to see their IDs. The man asked about their nationality and they tried to mumble a reply and avoid handing over their papers. Then, by a lucky chance and for no obvious reason, just as he was about to take their IDs his attention was attracted by some other men over to their left. He turned and walked towards them, ordering Abu Fakhry and Abu Yaseen to stay where they were. The bus driver, who had got out of his bus and was standing nearby, whispered urgently to them, 'Go, go, get away from here immediately or you will be picked up.' They managed to run to their car, which must have been a strain for both of them, for Abu Fakhry has a heart problem and Abu Yaseen has bad legs. They then threw themselves into their car and drove away. They saw similar incidents occurring all the way to our house, so it was entirely possible that they could still have got caught. Abu Fakhry stopped at our house for just long enough to give us some tomatoes and then hurried home as quickly as possible, vowing never to venture out again.

Yet another person passed by the Abu Huntash house to warn people not even to ride a bicycle outside. He said that hundreds were being picked up and taken away by the Iraqis. Nadr and I had another argument about what to do if the army came back to the museum. I insisted that this time I should go down and open the door and he should get into an air-conditioning duct. He disagreed. We just have to hope for the best.

[Much later on we learned that my older brother-in-law's 17-year-old son had been plucked off his doorstep, pushed inside a bus full of other Kuwaitis and driven through the bombing to a prison in Basra. He was lucky to have survived, for apparently there were also some Iraqis on the bus. They ran into some very heavy bombing and the Iraqis got out to find shelter, but refused to let the Kuwaitis leave.

They died but the Kuwaitis survived, even if only to end up in prison. My brother-in-law's son was released by the opposition some three weeks later, after which he had had to find his own way back to Kuwait, mainly on foot.]

6.30 p.m.
The flares are burning like fury and the sky is as red as blood. It looks just like Dante's inferno.

Saturday 23 February 1991
It again looks and feels like a scene from hell. The air smells strongly of petrol and the sky to the right of the water tanks (Nathem is still sitting atop one) throbs and pulsates with a red heat. I think it must be guns and planes that have been booming away, but at about five minute intervals and on a far more regular basis are what sound like explosions, which make me wonder whether they are blowing up more oil wells out in the desert. We are completely shrouded in black greasy smoke. The district beyond us can barely be seen and even Nathem and the water tanks are disappearing from sight. Through all this, a weak sun shows its face watery now and again. Bombs are falling somewhere and the insides of both houses rumble, thud, shake and jar and every now and again all the windows blow open, especially in Ziad's house. Nadr's eyes are aching and becoming swollen from the petrol fumes, and mine are somewhat sore, while everyone else feels ill in some form or another. Two young men have been taken off the street from one of the roads just behind us. We now barely put a nose out of doors: I dare not even walk 50 yards across to the mosque. I see absolutely no indication that Iraq is considering a withdrawal, though I did hear that the ordinary soldier is now petrified. Good.

8.23 p.m.
The Bayan Palace seems to be on fire once more and is burning really ferociously. This time there are no fire engines and no wailing police cars or vans, though it is possible that they have all been removed or smashed. Judging from the sky, the oil fires out in the desert are even worse than yesterday. The sky could not possibly throb more or become any redder than it is now. There still seem to be a good many

army vehicles going along both roads. Jeeps, lorries and even tanks tear up and down. Where do they get their petrol? Nathem and Kathem are still up there, but the soldiers around us seem to be flying to and fro. I have little idea of what is happening now. We did see some TV and the CNN report on the raid on Baghdad, but the electricity is flickering more than ever. We are saving the radio batteries for when it goes altogether.

Sunday 24 February 1991
The land war began at about 4.00 a.m. Oh how exciting! I do not know what will happen to us all, but at least we would die happy in the knowledge that Iraq has been ousted.

The Allies have retaken Failaka Island. The poor people of Failaka, how they suffered from being thrown off their island in the early days of the invasion. We think it was probably severely bombarded by Coalition warships a few days ago. I went up onto the roof to see if I could see anything, but no matter how hard I looked, all I could really see were explosions and black cloud.

The electricity has cut out completely and, as far as I can see, this holds true for the whole of Kuwait. The big substation in Fehaheel Road just beyond the bridge has been blown up by the Iraqis and is burning away fiercely. Behind me over in the direction of the Mubarak Hospital is another large fire. All of them are crackling and blazing away brightly. It seems hard to believe, but the flames from the substation are so strong that the metal is reacting as if the whole structure were made of paper, with machinery just crumbling away under the intensity of the fire. If I stand on top of the roof and listen in the direction of Ahmadi, I think I can hear the roar of the oil fires burning, though it may equally be the sounds of planes — it is a deep subterranean rumbling. We can hardly see anything because of the darkness and smoke.

Later on in the morning
There is no actual bombing at present, just the occasional sound of artillery fire. Neither Kathem nor Nathem (I can barely see that far) is at his post, though their guns are there. It is also raining quite hard in a drizzly sort of way. A steady throbbing sound from the direction of

Ahmadi can be heard above the noise of the army Jeeps tearing by on the Fifth Ring Road.

We are all praying for the Allied soldiers as they advance. Every now and again thunderous shaking and rattling rocks the houses. There are massive black clouds in the sky and the ones from the substation are billowing down the road in swirls. One can sometimes see rain clouds high above them, which are quite white in comparison with those from the oil fires.

Now we really have no idea at all what is going on. There is a ban on military news and what the Iraqis are really thinking we cannot imagine. Most people are firmly shut up indoors.

3.00 p.m.
As it became even darker and nastier we could see an enormous fire across the Fifth Ring Road in Bayan. We had no idea if it came from a petrol station, an ammunition dump or what, but it went up with a mighty explosion, shaking the ground, and sparks have been flying spectacularly for hours.

The radio says there are now possibly 300 oil-well fires burning.

The food in the refrigerator is starting to melt, but fortunately everyone had some days' warning so ate or gave away all they could beforehand.

Monday 25 February 1991 [Kuwait's National Day]
It is dark and black, but humid rather than warm. From the top of the roof it is still possible to hear the roar from the oilfields. I am sure that is what it is.

Now we have no water, no electricity, no gas, no petrol and no food. I suppose, if necessary, we will all have to do what the British and American embassies did — dig a well.

I gave the Saluki the remainder of some fatty meat and he promptly proceeded to bury it in three different places. As he is starving and emaciated that did not seem a sensible thing to do.

By mid-morning the ground was once again shaking from a variety of strong explosions.

From what we could see from the top of the roof this afternoon, we think that the Regency Palace Hotel on the seafront may have been set alight. Further along the coastline there are all kinds of spirals and plumes of dark smoke and cloud. They seem to be extending in the opposite direction as well, though what they all mean, we cannot say. Besides, there is so much black cloud and drizzle about that it is difficult to tell exactly what belongs to what. Amongst the various sounds, explosions and noises, we can still hear those very regular ones, which we think may be originating from the oilfields.

Tuesday 26 February 1991

What an unbelievable night! There was a sustained, deafening, tempestuous barrage with no let-up the entire time. It was so bad that I did not bother to undress and now and again I shot up ready to run for the basement. Once, when it seemed as if the room might cave in, I threw myself into a corner. The windows shook and the bathroom door nearly fell off its hinges. Every now and again I walked around the house and climbed to the top of the roof to look out, but although the sky was red, it was still very dark with no lighting of any kind. As usual, Nadr did not sleep, but remained watching and listening to everything. He misses his computers, but since there is no electricity there is nothing he can do about it. His eyes still hurt but seem less swollen. For want of anything more suitable, we each kept some heavy iron bars by our sides, which we intended to use if necessary. They would be useless against RPGs, but it makes one feel better to have them.

It was a bizarre night. The red and orange sky throbbed above the oilfields. One could barely hear the roar of the wells on fire (if that is what it was) through the intense and continuous barrage, the hiss and whine of rockets. It felt as if we were all in an upturned bowl of noise. The barrage lit up the lower sky with a blinding white light and blood red flashes that occasionally exploded in sparks. Beneath all that tumult and around us through the entire night was this loud undercurrent of rustling, shuffling and muttering, generating a feeling of frantic hurry. Though not that much could be seen because of the lack of light, the Fourth and Fifth Ring Roads seemed alive with the sound of engines, the rumble of tanks, jeeps, lorries, vans, the movements of anything and everything on wheels.

The closest analogy I can think of to what we could all hear is in the poem of *The Pied Piper of Hamelin*:

You heard as if an army muttered;
And the muttering grew to a grumbling;
And the grumbling grew to a mighty rumbling;
And out of the houses the rats came tumbling.

It was announced on the news early this morning that 500 wells had now been blown up and that many buildings in Kuwait were on fire, so presumably much of what we saw in our district could be seen in all the other parts of Kuwait as well.

As soon as it grew light enough I went downstairs and outside to take my daily look at Kathem. Trailing at the bottom of our road, out past the fence on the other side, a string of dispirited Iraqi soldiers could be seen, with heads down and guns flopping by their sides.

Kathem *and his gun* had gone, disappeared: all that remained were some bricks on the edge of the wall. As I stared about me, I thought I heard a woman ululating in the distance. I ran round the other corner to look at the mosque and someone said happily, 'It's clean now.' I think they were unearthing a Kuwaiti flag. I do believe Kuwait may be FREE — FREE — FREE.

We are still not quite sure. There is some shooting and planes are flying overhead.

10.00 a.m.

Very cautiously Nadr and I set off down the road past the apparently empty Iranian school (we half expected to get shot at and went very carefully round corners) and then we came to the side of the New English School. Its big old wooden side door was half open. We went round the corner and, always orderly, decided to enter through the main gate at the front of the building. Nobody seemed to be inside. We stepped in and saw a scene the likes of which I hope never to see again.

Outside, directly in front of the gate, were some of the foxholes that the soldiers had dug, with broken glassware from the school laboratories spilling out of them in all directions, as well as bits of material, and papers and files of all types. On top of one pile was an Afghan stringed instrument that had been on display in one of the cases beside the steps going down to the theatre. Immediately outside the gates were numerous individual bundles that had been left behind by the soldiers. It became obvious that what we had been hearing all last night were the sounds of men fleeing in deadly fear and panic. These men had been expecting a lorry to take them away, but they had been deserted by their officers and so eventually had to run, leaving behind all their pitiful stolen goods. I looked at the bundles with their bits of cheap material for a wife, a plastic toy for a child, a child's dress, an assortment of other stolen goods for a mother. There was even a secondary school yearbook lying on top of one pile.

I felt bitter anger and a deep unwilling pity for the ordinary people who had no doubt been forced into this position. But then I thought of the thousands of Kuwaitis who had been imprisoned, tortured, beaten and had their country brutally devastated. I thought of the hostages and the thousands (millions if one counts dependants) of other nationals who had had their lives ruined by the actions of these selfsame people, these people who were incapable of standing up and saying *no* to a vicious dictator and his henchmen, who cheered and demonstrated to order and who behaved so brutally and aggressively towards others. The turmoil of my emotions when I stared at (and photographed) those bundles made this one of the most devastating moments of my life.

Complete and utter chaos reigned both inside and outside the school. There was nothing, absolutely nothing, left unsmashed, untorn, unripped, unsodden. Cupboard doors hung from their hinges at crazy angles, desks were tipped broken on their sides. In the nurse's clinic the army had thrown the bed, screen, sterilizer and all the files into the yard through the unopened windows. Spilling down the stairs almost like a lava-flow, were papers, the remains of books and stationery covered in spray paint, urine, excrement and, in some places, chicken blood and feathers. No computers remained and the instruments from the music department lay scattered all over the school, either in pieces or, in one case, as a flattened effigy. The rest had just disappeared. One of the physics prep rooms just about typified it all, with every single instrument smashed and lying in piles on the floor pressed ankle-deep against the door so that it was impossible to get inside. Pipes were shattered and even the toilets had piles of paper and bits and pieces stuffed down them. In some parts of the school the toilet bowls had disappeared, while the changing rooms in the large gymnasium no longer had shower heads or even pipes. Even the big cricket net that had hung down part of the hall had gone. I wondered in passing if it now decorated a bunker or a personnel carrier.

From the state of the small gymnasium it was evident how much of a hurry the soldiers had been in when they left, for still alight on top of one of the battered vaulting horses stood a half-burned candle and there were some socks hanging on a line. A refrigerator from another part of the school (with its door hanging loose) seemed to have been used as a cupboard, for all its electrical parts had been taken away and it contained some pots. We walked carefully because there were guns lying around, as well as bullets and other munitions; and for all we knew there could be mines as well. The first thing we needed to do was to try and shut and secure the main doors, for, like everything else, they were dangling broken from their hinges. There were a number of heavy objects lying in the yard (from the gymnasiums and laboratories) that could be pushed against them.

Just as we finished barricading what we could, there was a sudden resounding crash and about ten heavily armed young men kicked open the main gate and poured Rambo-style inside.

'What the hell are you doing?' I bawled, already upset by what I had seen around the school.

They turned out to be from a Resistance group (I knew one of them quite well) and were coming to check the building for possible mines and explosives. I replied that I was very grateful for this, but would prefer them not to kick in gates and doorways, for enough damage had already been done. I did not wish closed doors to be booted in yet again. The young men charged around the building with their guns at the ready and eventually drifted away, once more leaving the gates open to the wind. Shooting could still be heard and in fact there seemed to be quite a lot around the bridge section across the road. Further in the distance were sounds of much heavier gunfire.

Nebila and Randa had taken their car out and gone on what we considered a rather daring drive, for in our area at least we were not completely sure that the Iraqis had gone. They said that further away in the next district people were dancing in the streets and that everyone had headed straight for Saddam's portraits and torn them down. We too had had our little celebration and I photographed Nadr tearing down Saddam's photograph from a wall in the administration block.

One of our neighbours passed by looking very worn and limping slightly. His brother had been horribly tortured to death by the Iraqis a few months previously.

The Iraqi retreat appeared to be a huge, undignified rout. According to the radio, soldiers were surrendering in ever-increasing numbers. I suppose that this is what Ziad and the other Kuwaiti interpreters would be helping to cope with out in the desert.

Kuwait was once more FREE, FREE, FREE and we all breathed an enormous and relieved thank you to the Allied forces.

10

Freedom

THE next day, when the Allies had reached the town, the entire population of Kuwait poured into the streets carrying flags and banners and pictures of the Amir and Crown Prince. If these had been found during the occupation the consequences would have been severe, but people hid them anyway in the hope of liberation. Everyone headed towards the American and British embassies near the Kuwait Towers along the seafront. They drove in cars they managed to hide or save from the Iraqis. They had made banners and posters with 'Thank you President Bush', 'We love you Margaret Thatcher' and, across a bridge, a huge one read 'Uncle Bush, France and Britain'. A bit of petrol was siphoned from here and there (it was still unavailable) and, with great honking and hooting, everyone rolled along the streets and cheered and clapped the Coalition tanks and personnel carriers as they rumbled triumphantly into Kuwait. In the middle of the road near the Egyptian Embassy some Egyptians sang and danced under a large banner.

A huge mass of leaping, dancing and slightly scruffy humanity shifted and swayed outside the embassies. A fine black drizzle was falling, but there was little water to spare for washing. Squatting against a wall at the back of the American Embassy, with a couple of marines guarding them, were 30 or 40 Iraqi soldiers. One could guess what their thoughts were as they drew heavily on their cigarettes and stared at the rejoicing crowd of Kuwaiti men, women and children. Everyone was far too busy blowing kisses at, or talking to, the American soldiers to take any notice of them.

When people were not congregating around the various Coalition embassies, they drove about Kuwait. The mess and destruction left behind was incredible. Some of it was much the same as in the school, but it was often even worse, especially when attempts had been made to burn out the buildings as well. All the hotels had suffered, some very badly, and we had been right about the Regency Palace: it had been set alight. What stood out was the spite and pointlessness of what had been done. We were also struck by the staggering quantities of ammunition (bullets of all sizes and shapes, mortars, guns, RPGs, cluster bombs, every conceivable type of death-dealing weapon) lying around in private houses, along the beaches and streets, in public buildings, dug into the ground, or spewing out of the hundreds of bunkers all over the country. Hundreds, perhaps thousands, of cases, often still lying unpacked in ammunition crates, were labelled 'GHQ Royal Jordanian Army'. The amount of money wasted on army equipment just beggared the imagination.

The happiness of being liberated was tempered by the knowledge that so many Kuwaitis had been abducted by the Iraqis, especially during the last few days of the occupation. In one district alone, Nuzha, it was estimated that at least one person from every household had been taken prisoner. And in 1992 some 800 had yet to be returned. There were thousands of cases of torture and rape in the detention centres that had been set up in public buildings and private houses. Entire families had been taken to prison in Iraq, where they lived on small amounts of foul water and bread and slept on crowded cement floors with no toilet facilities.

For a short while, which to us seemed endless, law and order in Kuwait completely broke down. It was particularly frustrating at the time and people rather unrealistically believed that the government-in-exile would be able to arrange supplies of water, light and food. They thought that no one was better equipped to assess the situation than people inside the country who had spent the past seven months organizing relief for the needy, but that their views were not being taken into account and, as a result, little was being done to alleviate conditions. One very annoyed lady who had distributed parcels during the occupation in the end took matters into her own hands by loading her van with packaged chickens and bread and driving to every house to distribute rations.

Some people had expected the government-in-exile, although a civilian government, to sweep into the country with the liberating military forces, though this was unrealistic and impractical. They remained depressed at what they perceived as a lack of concern for those who had suffered so much.

The whole country was in a total shambles, everything overcast by the heavy black pollution of the massive oil fires. For a short while no one could imagine how it would be possible to begin again, how normal business could recover, or even how people could return to the country. In fact, such were the shortages of everything that people outside Kuwait did have to wait for a further period before they were allowed back in.

Nadr acquired a pair of Iraqi night glasses and, with some sense of anticipation (for they are amazing, with night turning to day through a strange yellowish glow), he set off to take a look at the school. To his horror he saw two men in uniform, scarves covering their faces, creeping around with filled sacks slung over their shoulders. There was nothing he could do about it because they were both armed. This kind of thing was typical of that period and it was dangerous to venture out, even during the daytime. Iraqi soldiers left behind by their compatriots were holed up in empty houses. The remaining Palestinians, for at least 250,000 must have left during the period of the occupation, hardly dared to venture outside. Undoubtedly unpleasant incidents occurred; they could not be condoned but were understandable.

Looking back over comments in my journal during this difficult and unpleasant time, I am amazed at how fast even government institutions managed to revive, how law and order began to be restored. We complained about the government and its officials, but they did succeed in bringing order out of total disorder much faster than one might have expected.

The first thing that needed our attention was the school. In that mangled, sodden mess there were no brushes, rubbish bags or cleaning cloths. Where did one begin? I remembered the saying that everything starts with the first piece of paper picked up.

Some of our staff came in and, after staring at the amount of damage in their classrooms with horror, gallantly offered to help. It was an impossible job for about 12 people. But the whole country was in the same state and everyone had to begin somewhere.

As we tried to organize ourselves, the cultural attaché from the French Embassy, Monsieur Bourlon, came by to see how the museum had fared. His flat had been completely destroyed and his 20-year-old collection either smashed or stolen. Shortly after his visit a request was made by the French Army to use the school as a barracks. The site was ideal because it was near the embassy, could accommodate a large number of soldiers and had space outside for tanks, lorries, tents and all the accoutrements of a modern army.

That seemed a splendid idea. It would be a small way of thanking some of the people who had liberated Kuwait. Then I thought of the appalling mess both inside and outside and explained this to the commander.

'Let us go and see,' he suggested. So climbing into his jeep we spun off round the block to take a look. As the jeep drew up at the main gate I could see that some more men had jumped over the fence and were roaming about the yard.

Peering past the commander at the wheel, I growled, 'Who are those bloody men in the yard?' My language had not been improved by the occupation.

Impassively the commander glanced over and said, 'They are the French Army, Madame.'

Even the commander seemed shocked by the sight of the ruined educational equipment strewn everywhere, but was calm and unfazed by the problems of clearing it up sufficiently for use as a barracks. He estimated it would take about three weeks of hard work, which proved to be correct. It was an unpleasant job, with the staff and some 200 soldiers struggling with filthy files and wrecked furniture and with everyone pretending not to notice the particularly noxious rooms. They tended to be left to the unfortunate French soldiers! Most of the rubbish, endless loads of it, was shovelled into trucks and burned on fires outside the building. Some things could be saved, but not much. It was a painful job made better by the cheerfulness of the commander, the colonel and their men. Everyone worked from first light until darkness began to fall and we could no longer see anything.

Tanks, personnel carriers and heavy equipment began to line the front and sides of the school and big shower tents for the soldiers were hauled up. It was at this point that we began to consider what, if anything, should be done about the school year beginning in September 1991. There was no way of knowing if we would even have any pupils. Could people return to Kuwait? Could equipment be obtained in time? And, most importantly, would or could our staff return? The queries were endless and few answers were available. Fortunately we had access to the French telephones and fax systems and, by now in touch with my husband and the director, we decided that even one pupil would be sufficient to reopen school and, come what may, we would plan to open on 14 September 1991. There was a joyful reunion when my husband (and soon Ziad) landed in Kuwait on a French military plane, for we had been unsure that we would ever meet again. Shortly afterwards the director arrived to assess equipment for a somewhat theoretical student body. It was strange for my husband and Mr Rodgers to find their offices inhabited by a commander and colonel respectively and to have to have a pass to enter the premises.

The school did open on the set date, though the months from March to September were full of hair-tearing incidents and excitements. We never really doubted that we would somehow manage to be sufficiently prepared for the beginning of the school year. The French Army erected a large tent on the sand outside the school and a notice saying 'New English School — Registration' went up at its entrance. We sat there for the next few months with some retrieved pencils and application forms, answering questions and sometimes wondering if we were mad even to consider reopening. Gradually, after some months and encouraged by improving conditions as Kuwait slowly became more like its old self, other schools also began to prepare for their school year.

Among the most visible and shocking signs of the destruction wrought upon Kuwait by Iraq were the more than 730 oil fires raging out in the desert and heavily polluting not just Kuwait but the whole Gulf. The reality in the oilfields was staggering: although we had all seen the pictures in magazines and on television, nothing quite prepared one for the real thing.

It was evil, dramatic, frightening, a prime example of the worst side of human nature. The fires themselves, each different from the others, were compulsively beautiful; one could not avoid recognizing that. With a jet engine roar, red and yellow flames, alive with spears of blinding white and even shimmering green, shot into the sky, topped by black, swirling, acrid clouds of smoke. Some fires, more puffy smoke than flame, hissed into the air, while beads of flickering fire leapt hazardously across the lakes of oil, making it deadly dangerous for the firefighters working to extinguish them. Once, after a visit to the fires, I drove back to Kuwait singing and in a light-headed mood, wondering if it had been brought on by something in the smoke.

Our first trip to the oil town of Ahmadi was disquieting, for there, once again, were the smashed and looted houses, the ammunition, mines and mortars, and the greasy black roads full of defunct tanks. Everything — trees, sand, houses — was streaked with oil. Oil storage tanks had collapsed in on themselves; the main and once attractive office of the Kuwait Oil Company was shattered, its roof fallen in. Overall was a deathly silence, enhanced by the umbrella of deep, dark cloud hanging over it. Those who had remained suffered badly, for the damage to the electricity and other services took much longer to clear up.

One particular fire on the outskirts of the residential area near the main road was both beautiful and dangerous because, drawn to it in fascination, people had a tendency to drive too close. It roared straight up into the sky, a vicious orange and red with a silvery green at its base. At its peak began the great rolls of umbrella-like black and grey cloud. Even at a respectable distance the heat of the fire could be felt on the windows and inside the car. Lying in the sand further down, on the other side of the road, was the taut dried carcass of a once-handsome gazelle. Taken from the small Ahmadi zoo, its slender feet tied roughly together with rope, it had been beaten and then blasted through the head with a shotgun. It now lay in the sand, slowly becoming 'dust to dust'.

Now the fires are out, long before it was thought they could possibly be, but the desert is still dangerous with ordnance hidden by shifting sands, and oil lakes still disfigure the ground. Nevertheless, Kuwait is recovering, and it is now hard to explain to visitors and newcomers just what it was like immediately after the liberation, for they think people are exaggerating. As an old Kuwaiti remarked not long ago, in his *attar* (perfume) shop, which like everything else had been robbed and smashed, 'The soul has been wounded.' The scars from that will always remain. But the people, the tough descendants of merchants, Bedouin and pearl divers, will get on their feet once more and, with luck and determination, they will overcome all their tribulations.

Index